IN PUBLIC RECORD

A JOURNEY TO THE TRUTH OF A MURDER AND TRIAL

MICHAEL KELLY

WILDBLUE
PRESS

WildBluePress.com

IN PUBLIC RECORD published by:
WILDBLUE PRESS
P.O. Box 102440
Denver, Colorado 80250

WILDBLUE PRESS is registered at the U.S. Patent and Trademark Offices.

ISBN 978-1-970361-02-5 Hardcover
ISBN 978-1-970361-03-2 Trade Paperback
ISBN 978-1-970361-01-8 eBook
Cover design © 2025 WildBlue Press. All rights reserved.

Interior Formatting and Book Cover Design by Elijah Toten
www.totencreative.com

IN PUBLIC RECORD

CONTENTS

FOREWORD

Gene was gone. I hadn't seen him in years, had drifted away. I got a text with a link to the funeral home's website, and figured out it must have been from one of his daughters. I shed some tears, then began to laugh with memories. I stood in a church for his service and watched the emotions and tears of his big, loving family. Deaths and funerals can make you reflect on so many things; maybe that's the natural purpose. Presence, absence, mortality, time, love, family all run through the mind. It's a reminder of the fundamental truths of this existence. Questions and regrets can plague your reflections. What did I do? Did I do the right things? Was there something I could have done? Is there something I could do?

How do we treat our departed? We try our best to honor and memorialize, celebrate who they were, and express the inner mourning of their passing, the pain created by their absence. As a society, we create a duty to figure out answers if someone's life is lost unnaturally soon, taken from them by some means. We create a value towards those departed by acts of others, to determine why and try to bring some closure with justice. Would there be any less value or nobility if we could show a departed person had no wrongdoing?

There were two departed people who I shared an age group with but had never met. They always should have remained in my age group, just a slight bit older. The events of one night in September 1990 altered their paths forever, one ending and one being forever diverted. I had been fighting for them for a while with nothing to show and had let it go to nothing but frustration. Standing at Gene's funeral, I came to the decision there was one last thing I could do for these two souls. My days could come to an end having done nothing or having done something for them. Gene was one of the funniest people I ever met and one of my favorite and most dear coworkers I've ever had. Years before he made me laugh thousands of times and treated me like family, he was Detective Eugene Volk of the Cleveland Police Department's Homicide Unit. I was at his house one day and came across his retirement plaque laying around on a bench somewhere. I never forgot the inscription alongside his Homicide badge:

Under the Laws of Man, the highest of duties is to provide truth and justice when a fellow human being has had their life taken from them.

For Lisa, Kevin… and Gene.

Lisa Lee Pruett
5/29/1974—9/14/1990

Kevin Michael Young
01/27/1972—01/14/2017

Eugene Joseph Volk
3/3/1945—01/28/2025

The Poetess kissed The Painter above his eyes,
For it was not he caus'd her Earthly demise,
"Let us dwell no more on our stolen youth,
A Bard and a Constable shall tell our truth."

— a wayward constable

Flitting, floating, falling on the ground.
I freeze on children's eyelashes, and blur their altered vision of the world.
They see a different Earth than I. Of candy and playgrounds and eternal smiles.
I see the truth. Cold, bare trees stripped of life, and hard ground.

— Lisa Lee Pruett

3. "Bury the Lead" (03:33)

4. "Lisa Pruett Will Have Her Revenge on Coventry" (02:55)

5. "Come for the People, Stay for the Buildings" (1:15)

— *Clicks & Whistles* by Zapruder Point

CHAPTER 1 : TAKING AMY TO THE LIBRARY

It all started with a picture. At the bookstore one day, I came across a book in the local interest section with a picture that made me pick it up and purchase it without second thought. The book was *Amy: My Search For Her Killer* by James Renner. The picture was of Amy Renee Mihaljevic, victim of possibly the most heartbreaking unsolved murder in Northeast Ohio. The picture was branded in the consciousness of many throughout the region as it was shown nightly on every news broadcast for months while she was missing, lured out and captured by an unknown predator by a phone call. I can't think of any picture more seared into my mind, and countless others would agree. Her body was found months later in a farm field counties away, and her case has never been solved. It drove Renner to a cause and writing a book, and to me to purchase that book.

I enjoyed reading the book, and later would find a book by Renner on the disappearance of University of Massachusetts nursing student Maura Murray, very appropriately titled *True Crime Addict*. It was a very intriguing read, and I read the book twice over. Of the books I've read of Renner's, I think it was the best read, though he would later lament it and his time spent on it. It is truly an addictive case with no answer, as no possibility can be definitively pointed to nor definitively eliminated. In my twenties, I had been a police officer in a very small city, and had dreamed of being a detective, having one big case that drove me and solving it. I read or watched any subject on true crime thinking how I would handle it.

In early November 2023, I noticed a flyer at my library that Renner would be at the library one evening coming up. I figured I'd like to shake his hand and tell him how much I enjoyed the two books I had read. I might as well take my copy of *Amy* to get an autograph. If I could get a minute, I had just one question on each of the books, sort of a nod to the old detective show *Columbo*. I showed up that evening and saw Renner walk by near the front entrance. I checked a few things on the computer, then started to look around for him. I had thought it would be something like a book signing, but didn't see him anywhere. I asked a clerk at a desk where he was, and she told me he was giving a presentation downstairs in one of the auditorium rooms. I went downstairs and found a room with thirty to forty people sitting in chairs waiting as Renner began a presentation with a media projector on his newest book. I took a seat near the back.

His newest book was titled *Little, Crazy Children*, and dealt with the 1990 murder of Lisa Lee Pruett of Shaker Heights, Ohio, and the 1993 trial of former classmate Kevin Young. He referenced the Salem Witch Trials and Arthur Miller's *The Crucible* for the title, revealing that he believed that privileged teenagers in a wealthy suburb had guided a story, pointing the finger at Young to protect a friend. He thought Young was unfairly treated and tried on no real evidence, and for many years, thought Lisa's boyfriend had been the real killer. I had never heard of the case or the names, no recollection of the case like I immediately had with Amy. It would be the first time I would learn of the use of cough syrup as a recreational drug, imported into the teenage social circle relevant to the case by boyfriend Daniel Dreifort. Lisa was found stabbed to death after sneaking out of her house after midnight on a school night to visit her boyfriend at his residence. Others were invited to attend, and it was suspected to be a "Robo" party where cough syrup might be overdosed on to produce differing effects. Lisa's boyfriend had been released from psychiatric care the previous afternoon, and it was suggested he wanted to party that night.

Kevin Young was apparently a suspect because he was at a location where the plans for this get-together were openly discussed, and had some emotional problems. He had supposedly stated some threats against Dan and Lisa in the past. It did not seem like a random killing, and it was thought that the killer had to have a motive of anger against Lisa. Renner went on to profess his belief in Young's innocence, that there was no real evidence against him, though indicted and tried for the murder, which was covered by Court TV in addition to local media. Renner brought his presentation towards a close, turning his suspicion to another local no-good-nik, David Branagan, who he thought killed Lisa. He then blended another case in linking Branagan to the murders of newspaper editor Phillip Porter and his wife Dorothy, killed five years earlier and mere houses away from where Lisa was found. He transitioned to a cause of freeing Donald Soke, currently in prison for the murders of the Porters and a Lake County mother, believing Soke was a serial confessor imprisoned by questionable police work.

Soke's image was a blast from the past that made me flinch. I remembered images of his face on television, forehead tattooed with a spiderweb design. It seemed at the time, to myself (and I'm sure others), as a face of evil. A sibling of his moved into my neighborhood when we were youths, and eventually had to change their last name due to the notoriety. If I had remembered Amy and Soke so well, why did I have no recollection of the case of Lisa Pruett? It seemed like an interesting enough case, and because of enjoying Renner's last two works, I figured I'd give this a read.

I waited at the end of the line, hoping to get Renner to myself to ask a couple questions. I got the autograph on *Amy* I was looking for, and began to ask questions as he packed up. The person he suspected as Amy's killer seemed to be a gay man to me, making less sense. He said that was what an agent told him once, but it could be irrelevant in child predator cases. I threw in a question about the Maura Murray investigation. After riding the elevator up and complimenting his work again, I realized something: I had forgotten to buy the book.

This book is not intended to be competition or critique of *Little, Crazy Children*, rather a sequel and culmination of the efforts of Renner. I highly recommend the book and others of his. Renner is a gifted writer and gives a wider and more in-depth view of the people and situations surrounding the case, and gives good homage to those involved, especially Lisa and Kevin. This book will take a more targeted approach, looking for that one right path, cutting through the things that don't matter to get to what really matters. If it begins to sound more like a police report, please realize that the only way I can tell this story is from how I lived it as an investigator with the right police training and a little bit of experience. Perhaps reading *Little, Crazy Children* first would be recommended. I've read it at least seven times, if that helps. I stand on the shoulders of Renner and others to give you a journey to the truth.

CHAPTER 2 : YOUNG LOVE

A bicycle cut through the night air just after midnight in the suburb of Cleveland known as Shaker Heights, Ohio. It had just become September 14, 1990, a school night for sixteen-year-old Lisa Lee Pruett, now a junior at Shaker Heights High. She was sneaking out of her home to visit her first love, boyfriend Daniel Dreifort, also sixteen, at his home at 2940 Lee Road. They had formed a romance during a school band trip to Germany earlier in the year, and had not gotten the chance to see each other much of late.

Daniel had surprised her the previous day, a Thursday. He had been hospitalized at the Cleveland Clinic in a psychiatric ward for the previous thirty-five days, and Lisa was not aware he was going to be discharged early. Lisa had sent him plenty of letters while he was away, filled with her endless expressions. Daniel's father, Robert Dreifort, worked as an administrator at the Cleveland Clinic, and had put Daniel in the facility for reasons uncertain. After his discharge around two p.m., Daniel was able to arrive home, then bike to school to surprise Lisa later in the school day. It was progressing as a fantastic day for Lisa, who, exhilarated at being able to see Daniel, was going to take her driving test, achieving the important teenage milestone of earning and receiving her driver's license.

Daniel visited friends, then returned home to eat dinner. After dinner, his parents went out, and neighbor Kim Rathbone cut his hair, as Daniel trusted her with that duty. Friend Kenny Workman came over the Dreifort residence. Kenny, in addition to being friends with Daniel, was dating Daniel's older sister, Deborah. Deborah was already away and in classes at Ohio University.

Later in the evening, Lisa was driven over to Dan's house by her father, Gary Pruett, after her flute lesson. Her father stayed in the car while Lisa paid Dan a very brief visit. Dan recalled it being around nine p.m. After parting ways, Dan recalls talking on the phone with Lisa at some point in the next hour. They discussed her sneaking out to come over his house late that night, sometime around 12:30. Dan mentions having Lisa throw a rock at his window.

Lisa was not the only invitee to the Dreifort house later that night. Daniel had wanted a bigger group of friends to gather that evening, in addition to Lisa and Kenny. He had contacted school friends Chris Jones and Daniel Messinger while visiting the school. It was speculated that Dan wanted to celebrate his release with a "Robo" party. It was something introduced to the local teens as a cheap and available recreational drug. Overdosing on Robitussin or other brands of cough syrup had differing effects according to statements later made by those interviewed in this case. The active ingredient, dextromethorphan, can have toxic effects, according to the website for American Addiction Centers. Of the many effects of intoxication and overdose listed for the drug, dissociative episodes, audio and visual hallucinations, nausea, impaired motor functions, agitation, anxiety, paranoia, blacking out, restlessness, blurred vision, and convulsions stand out. Drowsiness is also listed as an effect, later asserted by Kenny. It seems like a very wide range of effects for a substance. The site states that effects start fifteen to thirty minutes after ingestion and can last for three to six hours. It is also listed as habit forming.

Kenny Workman had departed at some time estimated to be around ten o'clock. He would travel to a local Arabica coffee shop to hang out for a bit. This would later become a critical focal point in regards to who had knowledge of Dan's planned get-together that night. Kenny was in the presence of Stanley Kramer, Kevin Young, Holly Robinson, and David Branagan at the Arabica shop, and had spoken of the get-together in front of those people. Kenny had taken Dan's bicycle to the shop, and was to pick up cigarettes for Dan and drop them off back at the Dreifort house. Kenny had originally learned of Dan's release from Ken Mitsumoto while at the same coffee shop earlier in the day, and called Dan. Kenny talked with Kevin Young for around forty-five minutes, then returned the bicycle and cigarettes to Dan around eleven o'clock. Dan wanted Kenny to spend the night at the house, as he had done many times, but Kenny departed for the Rapid Transit stop at around 11:15, finally arriving at his residence after midnight. He spoke to girlfriend Deb Dreifort on the phone after midnight.

It seemed that everyone else Dan invited over was reluctant to venture out on this particular school night, except for girlfriend Lisa. Chris Jones, Rebecca Boatright, and others all decided not to come over for whatever reasons. Daniel watched the evening news, then retired to his bedroom to listen to music and put things away after his return from the hospital. Deb would call home shortly after midnight and the family would take turns speaking on the phone with her.

Then something shook the still night as screams were heard outside around 12:30. Dan and his father Robert both reported hearing the screams. Dan's bedroom and that of his parents, Robert and Jean, connected through a shared bathroom. Robert asked Dan if he heard the screams, and they both had. Dan had shoes on, so Robert suggested he go outside to see what was going on. Robert had been naked and needed to throw some clothes on to follow Dan outside. Daniel went out to the edge of their property but did not see anything. He suggested to his father to call the police, but they would reason that there was nobody there and nothing to be done. Another resident in the area had called police; a unit drove by the area and found nothing.

The Dreiforts returned to their respective bedrooms, but Dan soon realized he had forgotten something. Lisa was planning on coming over around that time, and he became fearful the screams had been his love. He snuck back out of the house to check around for her. After walking just south of his property on the Lee Road sidewalk, he found a bicycle in the unkempt vegetation bordering the sidewalk, essentially the corner boundary of the northwest intersection of Lee and South Woodland Roads. It was essentially a side yard that looked more like a backyard and constituted the property of 16401 South Woodland. He recognized the bicycle as Lisa's, and propped it up against the saplings growing next to the sidewalk. Dan then ran inside to call Lisa's house; he did not hear anyone pick up before the answering machine and hung up. He then dialed 911 without his parents' knowledge to report that he feared the screams may have been Lisa.

Police responded to the scene. Dan relayed the story about the screams and how Lisa was supposed to come over around that time and he had forgotten. The officer initially reported that Dan said he didn't hear the screams. Dan led him to the bicycle in the sidewalk vegetation. He said he had touched the bike to lift it up. Dan asked if he should notify his parents, and went back in the house to do so.

Multiple police units began searching the area. Officers searching the side yard of 16401 South Woodland soon came across the body of a young female. She had been stabbed to death. Her shirt was found pulled up over her brassiere. Her pants and panties were pulled totally off her left leg and down to her right ankle; her left shoe was pulled off and found close by, her right shoe remaining on. The body was not far from the bicycle on the other side of the high vegetation.

It was Lisa.

CHAPTER 3 : INVESTIGATION

It was a homicide, and that necessitated much more manpower and attention. The yards were sealed off as searches for evidence continued. Supervisors were contacted and detectives called in. So much work needed to be done, and needed to be coordinated. It didn't help that it was nighttime. The scene needed to be protected and searched. The neighborhood needed to be canvassed for witnesses. Pictures, statements, evidence, and notes all had to be taken.

It was noted that a Hawaiian Punch bottle, the *Plain Dealer* Sunday magazine, and a brown paper bag with a possible footprint in blood were located near her body. Somewhere, a condom partially out of its packaging was located in one of the yards. Lisa's body was eventually transported to the Cuyahoga County Coroner's Office for examination and autopsy. Something unusual was noted: Dan Dreifort had returned to his bedroom to go to sleep. The Dreiforts invited officers into their residence. Later, it was determined the family all needed to be taken back to the Shaker Heights Police Station to make official statements. They were transported down the road to the station, and their statements were taken in the old-school method of being typed out by detectives, then signed by the witnesses.

An officer was sent to the Pruett residence. After knocking on multiple doors, Lisa's parents, Gary and Lynette, awoke and came to the front door. The officer asked if Lisa was home, and initially her father asserted that she was. When he was asked to double check, he found her bed empty. He was asked about her bicycle, and it was found her bicycle was gone as well. The Pruetts were transported to the Lee Road scene. Later, upon the family checking Lisa's room, it was found that a pink folding wallet was missing but her newly earned driver's license was still in the room.

At the Cuyahoga County Coroner's Office, Lisa's body was examined and her autopsy was officially noted to have been performed at 8:50 a.m. Multiple stab wounds, at least nineteen by count in the report, are noted of the head, neck, trunk, and right and left upper extremities. Abrasions and contusions are noted on her trunk. Abrasions and lacerations are noted on her right index and middle fingers. Contusion of the neck is further noted. Her cause of death is listed as homicide due to the multiple stab wounds and exsanguination. Most of her bleeding was internal; her left lung was punctured multiple times along with her aorta. One of the most important preliminary findings was there was no evidence of sexual assault, as her exposure might have suggested.

A great search began for someone with motive to do this to Lisa, someone with some internal reason to unleash such rage on an innocent, well-liked young girl. Kenny Workman had to be questioned, and was interviewed, and signed a statement as to his activities that day and night. Many people from Lisa's life were interviewed—neighbors, teachers, and schoolmates. All told of a wonderful young person. Attention would start to be given to the people who knew Lisa would be going over to Dan's house that night as it seemed much less likely to be a random crime of opportunity. Detectives would bring in and probe all those either invited to the Dreifort residence that night or who may have heard about the get-together somewhere like the Arabica coffee shop. Classmates and friends were questioned about anyone who might have that level of anger towards her and could have done that to Lisa. The first name that seemed to coincide with both possible knowledge of the get-together and possible threat or animosity toward either Lisa or Dan was Kevin Young. Kevin was regarded by many schoolmates as a bit of a "weird" kid in school. He had exhibited some emotional problems and had trouble with girls and dating. It was reported he made threats against Dan and Lisa in the past.

An undated police department memorandum found in files lists eight possible theories for Lisa's homicide. The first possibility listed was that of a random killing, a crime of opportunity. Seven names are then listed as potential killers of Lisa: Dan Dreifort, Kenneth Workman, Kevin Young, Christopher Jones, Becca Boatright, Robert Dreifort, and Stanley Kramer. The first possibility of a random killing is given astronomical statistical odds against it considering the circumstances surrounding the get-together and who knew about it, especially considering that Dan was unexpectedly released early and the idea of that get-together was formulated that afternoon or evening.

What is more clear by the dates is that police had already honed in on Kevin Young as a primary suspect by the following day. Kevin had already graduated from Shaker Heights High and was beginning classes at Ohio State University that coming Monday. Police wanted to search his residence and interview him before an impending trip to Columbus on Sunday. A search warrant was issued at one a.m. that Sunday morning, and a search of his house commenced at 1:57 according to records. A report states that Kevin was brought to the police station by his mother, Maryanne, for an interview at around 11:15 that Saturday night. Kevin was told that multiple people had reported he had made threats against Dan and Lisa that summer, and he was accused of killing Lisa. Kevin insisted he had only made threats against Dan, and they shouldn't have been taken seriously. Kevin stated that he had returned to his family residence a bit after eleven on the night of the 13th, and he tried to go to bed but ended up watching television, never going back out. The police report states that Kevin was smoking "deep drags" on a cigarette, and at one point, curled up into the "fetal position" when investigators left the room to observe him through a two-way mirror. On two occasions, he was noted as mouthing the words "no, no, no." Kevin was questioned about his sexual history and relationships with women. He made and signed a typed out statement and was picked up by his father, J. Talbot Young, at around 3:30 a.m. on the 16th. It should be noted now that Kevin's father was a prominent attorney and did not in any way preclude his son from being interviewed.

Kevin's signed statement strangely notes certain things on the days before and after the murder. He specifically stated that Kenny Workman told him it was supposed to be a "Robitussin" party at Dan's house that night, with Lisa and Chris Jones supposedly coming over. Kevin stated that his mother woke him the next day because Kenny was at his door. His mother had learned of the murder, and Kenny told him Lisa had been raped as well. Kevin goes on to state that he met up with Kenny around noon at Arabica, where Kenny became hysterical. He stated Kenny was worried people would think that he (Kenny) had killed Lisa and had left a knife at the Dreifort house. As they walked to The Shack, Kenny told Kevin that he thought Dan killed Lisa, and Kenny threatened to kill Dan if he found out it was true. Kenny was also worried about his own alibi, according to Kevin. Kevin goes on to state that Debbie Dreifort had come back into town from college upon hearing the news, and that he was a "wreck" until she got in. Kevin stated that Debbie was originally convinced her brother killed Lisa, and upon hearing rumors she was raped, worried that Dan's semen would be found inside her. Kevin even started to wonder if Kenny had been the killer, and had strangely killed Lisa because of a crush Kevin had on Lisa during a band trip. Near the end of his statement, Kevin said that after the five o'clock news came on, it was obvious Dan had not done it.

An extremely thick book could be written of all the statements made to police in this case. I will do my best to sift out the relevant and meaningful. I will say that there is no shortage of persons willing to state that Kevin was strange or disconcerting to them. There is also no shortage of people speaking well and lovingly of Lisa.

CHAPTER 4 : THE TRIP DOWN 71

In little more than ten days after Lisa's murder, the Shaker Heights Police decided the full efforts of their investigation was to be aimed at Kevin Young as the suspect. A team of seven officers was formed to head down to Columbus with aims of getting Kevin to confess to the murder. There was even a pep talk from the city prosecutor's office offering encouragement and cheering the efforts of this small task force. A second search warrant was drafted, this time for Kevin's Ohio State University dorm room. Detective Tom Kohansky would bring his polygraph equipment to administer the tests to Kevin, should he accept. The group headed down the road to Columbus, Interstate 71, on September 26.

Kevin was agreeable to the interviews and tests. He was taken to a local hotel where Shaker Heights officials had obtained rooms for the interviews and any polygraph tests. Kevin was interviewed for hours, long into the night, with breaks, and given cigarettes and soda. Kevin would never confess, and agreed to multiple polygraph tests. His father, attorney Tal Young, never discouraged him. At some point in the investigation, Kevin also gave blood, hair, and fingernail samples.

It was not an overly confrontational affair, and Kevin had been taken for food and given breaks for rest. It was said that it lasted over eighteen hours. Kevin was asked to imagine how the crime happened. He played along, but never confessed. At some point, it was suggested that Kevin would never be able to go back to Shaker Heights again. The whole thing had started to affect his mental health. He called home to his parents. His parents then decided to place him in Laurelwood mental health services for in-patient care, which lasted nearly three months.

Kevin's hospitalization was not the only thing that resulted from the Columbus trip. On September 28, Shaker Heights Police Chief Walter Ugrinic announced they had a suspect in the murder. The *Plain Dealer* headline on the 29th was "POLICE SAY ARREST NEAR." Ugrinic hoped to file charges "within a week," though he was not listed as being involved in either the crime scene or trip to Columbus. He stated the suspect was "under a doctor's care." The article also noted that Lisa was killed while attempting to visit a boyfriend, and that the police questioned the "boy" but declined to say if he was a suspect. The "boy" had reportedly attended a separate conference for Lisa's friends where police gave them the same information. It went on to say the "father" said he wasn't supposed to talk about the case, but that the "boy" had taken a polygraph test. When asked the results of the test, the "father" told the reporter, "You have to draw your own conclusions." Strangely, the crime scene evidence had not arrived at any laboratory as of the date of the article.

CHAPTER 5 : FAKE NEWS AND A LONE VOICE OF REASON

Some of us trace the first use of the term "fake news" not to any politician, but to comedian Norm MacDonald as host of the famous "Weekend Update" of *Saturday Night Live*. "And now, the fake news" would be MacDonald's usual lead-in for the comedic version of current events offered up on the late Saturday stalwart. Many would later believe that MacDonald's firing was due to the influence of certain powerful people who didn't care for his unabashed targeting of O.J. Simpson in his "Weekend Update" jokes before, during, and after Simpson's "trial of the century" for the murders of his former wife Nicole Brown Simpson and Ron Goldman. MacDonald gained much respect in the eyes of many for the whole ordeal, never wavering in his words. Kevin Young would have one prominent figure on television in the early days who was in his corner: a serious, respected journalist and commentator instead of a goofy comedian.

For the majority of Northeast Ohio, Cleveland's *Plain Dealer* has always been the main source of journalism and news, in addition to four or five local television stations offering news programs throughout the day. In researching old news footage covering the case, I found many of the familiar faces who Northeast Ohioans welcomed into their homes via their television sets—Ted Henry, Wilma Smith,

Leon Bibb, Tim Taylor, Romona Robinson, Carl Monday, and Paul Orlousky, among others—were all long-time institutions of the Cleveland television news scene who could be seen covering the case.

Kevin's name leaked somewhere to the media in the early days of the investigation. Old footage shows his picture on the newscasts, as well as an officer stationed outside his residence. At some point, the city of Shaker Heights put out a press release confirming the leaked reports; the name of the prime suspect was indeed Kevin Young. Footage aired on a local television station displayed the following text on the screen with letterhead in the background: "THE NAME OF THE PERSON WHO IS THE PRIMARY FOCUS OF THE INVESTIGATION HAS BEEN RELEASED (BY TV8)... WILL CONFIRM KEVIN YOUNG IS THE SUSPECT..." Additional screenshots read as follows, noting the underlined word: "BOYFRIEND IS NOT THE SUSPECT"(allusion to media questioning of Daniel Dreifort) "...Caused young man and his family ... severe emotional stress."

The media feeding frenzy continued to grow like wildfire, every station and paper carrying Kevin's name as the lone suspect. Allusions to emotional problems and statements made in the past regarding Lisa and Dan were distributed to the public. Conversely, Dan Dreifort and his family were explicitly excluded as suspects and protected to the media. This was all in a period of time where no forensic results were even close to being made available by the FBI Laboratory, which was utilized by many police departments of the era who did not have access to technologies such as DNA testing on a regional basis. It also appears to be months before crime scene photos were developed. It was very strange for a city to do either of these things regarding subjects such as Kevin and Dan during an investigation, and other prominent law enforcement officials made opinions insinuating that to reporters that made it into a *Plain Dealer* article. Shaker Heights Police Chief Walter Ugrinic, being interviewed by a news station, stated that his department's investigation was being conducted to the highest of standards and that he had "no problem" with the investigation being reviewed. It would be suggested that a "case" against Kevin was being made to important "key communicators" inside the Shaker Heights community by the police department. Detective Tom Kohansky was listed with "community relations" responsibilities in this case, in addition to administering polygraph examinations. The Young family needed a good criminal attorney, and were led to up-and-coming defense attorney Mark DeVan. DeVan would publicly start to rebut the case and allegations against Kevin.

DeVan started to push back at Shaker Heights and the media to the media. DeVan decried a smear campaign to reporters, and put out Kevin's alibi—he was home with his parents at the time of the murder. "They have interfered with our investigation and provided false information to the community," railed the attorney. He "blasted city officials for meeting with residents to outline their case" and accused the department of discouraging witnesses from speaking with defense investigators. He further accused them of suggesting that Kevin was not cooperating and put it out that Kevin spent eighteen hours with investigators without requesting an attorney, the profession of his own father. He chastised the media for leaking Kevin's name.

It was alluded to that a professional connection was stalling the case. Shaker Heights Mayor Stephen Alfred worked at the same firm as Kevin's father, Tal Young. One thing that should be noted from articles is that Shaker Heights handled felony cases differently than many other suburbs. The city's law department would form cases, then take them to the county rather than police working directly with assistant county prosecutors. The illness of City Prosecutor K.J. Montgomery and the delay of waiting for results on forensic testing from the FBI Laboratory were listed as primary obstacles.

A July 18, 1991, *Plain Dealer* article detailed a press conference called to announce that the investigation yield was "too weak" to seek an indictment. Ugrinic insisted police still had "the right suspect," alluding to the classmate with an unrequited crush on Lisa. DeVan shot back with threats of a civil lawsuit. County Prosecutor Stephanie Tubbs Jones, later elected to the United States House of Representatives, was said to have reviewed the case and decided not to take it to a grand jury. Assistant County Prosecutor Carmen Marino, who would later try the case, insisted the "law enforcement investigation of this case has been excellent" with no "indication that anything improper has been done in this case." Marino went on to state that the "suspect is not psychotic, but had a mental aberration consistent with an enraged murder." There was "no way to know" if the killer might seek another victim. Officials insisted that forensic testing results kept coming back with new questions, and that a "cycle" of questions and new tests were ongoing.

The Young family somehow found a champion, a voice of reason, in Cleveland's premier commentator, the late journalist Dick Feagler. Feagler was a long-time stalwart in print and television news, his charming crankiness earning the respect of peers and the public over many decades of service to Northeast Ohio. Feagler interviewed Kevin's parents, Tal and Maryanne, on his show and would give additional commentary on the case on live broadcasts. No words I can say or write can come close to those of the immortal Dick Feagler, so I will offer his commentary directly.

ANCHORMAN LEON BIBB: Shaker Heights officials are challenging DeVan to put his evidence his client is innocent on the table. Dick Feagler comments on that.

FEAGLER: Comments, comments, the whole commentary is in the last thing that Leon said. Since when is the lawyer of a kid who has been called a murderer challenged to prove the kid's innocent? It's supposed to work the other way around. If you claim somebody's a murderer, you're supposed to have to prove he's guilty. Somewhere in the Shaker Heights Law Department or Police Department or Prosecutor's Office, somebody must have a law book, or at least the Cliff Notes for a law book. Now if there's any challenging to be done, it's got to go the other way. I've never seen such a cavalier brush off of centuries of legal precedent just so that, what? So the voters of Shaker Heights will think their city is on the ball? There are two lives in this story. There is the life of Lisa Pruett, brutally ended, and there is the life of the young man the police are playing with. They hold a press conference. We know who killed her. The kid whose name we leaked out some months ago. You reporters all know it. Some of you are using it. Now we talk to him for eighteen hours without a lawyer and couldn't shake a story. We searched his room and couldn't find anything; we sent tissue samples to the FBI and they couldn't tell us anything, but he did it. Just take it from us. And if his lawyer thinks he didn't, we challenge him to prove it. A trial. No courtroom, no jury, no evidence, no lawyer present, no defendant present. A trial by press conference. A conviction by bluster. Something new? No, totalitarian countries, dictatorships, kingdoms have used those methods before. But the people of

Shaker Heights think they're living in America, and they ought to challenge their city officials to prove that.

A later commentary in 1991 by Feagler:

> More than a year has passed since sixteen-year-old Lisa Pruett was murdered in Shaker Heights, more than a year of agony for two families. The Pruett family, obviously, and the family of Kevin Young, nineteen, who Shaker Heights Police, at a press conference the likes of which I've never seen, fingered as their chief suspect in the murder. A couple of months ago, Tal and Maryanne Young, Kevin's parents, agreed to an interview with me. We ran it here on the news. In the interview, the Youngs said that their son was home with them the night of the murder. They insisted that the Shaker Police had no evidence and were, in effect, framing their son, Kevin, because they needed a suspect. Last night, Kevin Young came to the station to see me; he was badly upset. He said the strain of living under the unproven accusation of murder was devastating him, and it obviously was and it obviously would. When this investigation was new, hair and tissue samples were taken from Kevin Young and sent to the FBI crime lab to match with those found on the victim. The test results have come back, the Shaker Heights Police have not released them. It is time they did. If they have any evidence against Kevin Young, it is time for them to say so. If they have none, it is time for them to say that. What has been done in the Lisa Pruett murder case is not justice. The girl whose life is gone deserves better and so does the boy whose life is in ruin, and so do the citizens of this county.

CHAPTER 6 : THE HAM SANDWICH

There is a famous saying that has circulated in the legal profession for a long time: you (or I) can indict a ham sandwich. I first heard it in legal classes and would go on to hear it on television and in real life from confident or cynical attorneys. The saying relates to the relative ease of obtaining a criminal indictment in a case versus achieving a conviction. There is, by design, a much lower threshold of proof standard to be indicted by a grand jury than to be convicted by a trial jury and face serious consequences of imprisonment or worse. A grand jury basically hears the summary of the case and evidence up to that point and determines if there is enough cause for a person to be *charged* with a crime—not convicted. Up until a certain point, the case against Kevin didn't even seem like a sandwich to many; perhaps crumbs and a breadcrust at best.

Then something happened. A woman named Susan Lape, who had been a patient at Laurelwood at some point during Kevin's months of treatment there, was referred to Carmen Marino by an acquaintance of hers who worked in the justice system. A typed statement with the date July 24, 1991, lists Shaker Heights Detective Tom Gray as the official taking the statement. Lape stated that after watching the big press conference from the week before with Marino and Shaker Heights officials, she wanted to come forward with suspicious statements she said she heard from Kevin while in the in-patient treatment facility. Lape stated she inquired to Kevin as to the reason he was in the facility, and that he related, "Only my psychiatrist knows… as long as he never talks." Lape further recounted a more ominous statement made by Kevin: "They'll never find out who killed that girl. There were only two people there; one is dead and the other is never talking."

A year passed. Kevin tried another stint in college at a local university, then ended up working menial jobs, often painting houses. Then, in the fall of 1992, things ramped back up to the war footing they had been two years earlier. Another psychiatric patient treated in-house at Laurelwood came forward to give even more damning statements supposedly made by Kevin. Edythe Heinz made an official statement on September 19, 1992, that Kevin had shown her newspaper clippings of the murder coverage while both were in the facility. Heinz related asking Kevin directly, "Did you do it? Did you kill her?" She stated that Kevin simply answered "yes" without hesitation. She further related that she asked him why he had done it, and he replied, "I killed her because."

Focus went to people who had been around Kevin during his hospitalization, and fellow patients and staff at the facility. A number were interviewed and made official statements. Worker Anastasia Tressler related a statement made by Kevin of, "Well, maybe I did hurt the little girl."

Her notes later exhibited in court contained the following statement made by Kevin: "The torment will never end. I don't know, maybe the police are right. Maybe I did kill the girl. Maybe I do have three personalities, but I would know that, wouldn't I?"

The ham sandwich finally had a piece of two-year old bread and some meat on it. Police and prosecutors began to go to the media again, and a criminal indictment was finally pursued. The case was taken to a Cuyahoga County grand jury on November 19, 1992, and news of a "true bill" was published in the *Plain Dealer* on November 25. Grand juries have the options of a true bill, in which they agree there is enough cause to sustain charges against a person, and a no bill, in which they would decide there was not enough. There would be no relenting from Kevin, his family, and their legal team. No confessions, no plea negotiations, and no more trial in the court of public opinion. Kevin, his family, and Mark DeVan would deny any and all accusations, and fight to the bitter end.

There was a seemingly unending list of legal maneuvers on both sides before either side or the court could begin a real trial. Many motions had to be filed. Psychiatric and healthcare records had to be argued over to determine if they were proper, or prejudicial to be seen by a jury. Search warrants were contested, though they didn't seem to result in anything relevant. The sides fought over gag orders, with third-party news agencies wanting information. DeVan would argue that excessive pre-trial publicity would be prejudicial against his client, citing the famous trial of the century four decades earlier in the same court system of Sam Sheppard for the murder of his wife, Marilyn. Sheppard's eventual conviction was overturned partly based on the pre-trial publicity. DeVan further put out Kevin's cooperation to the media and the fact that his parents wanted to give interviews to police supporting his alibi.

DeVan argued for a very relatively low bond for a murder defendant: fifty thousand dollars. Kevin's lack of criminal record, ties to the community, scarcity of evidence, and the fact that he had not tried to leave the area were points DeVan argued to the judge setting bail. DeVan offered a new psychiatric report on Kevin that declared him competent.

Marino would not seek the death penalty for Kevin, rather a maximum of life in prison for aggravated murder. The *Plain Dealer* referred to Kevin as the "preppy house painter." Marino put it out that Kevin's doctors did not want to release Kevin, but were overruled by his family. DeVan quickly disputed that, saying Kevin was treated for depression, not incarcerated.

Judge James Sweeney would rule against any gag orders. Marino then sought to nullify any doctor-patient privilege to allow Kevin's psychiatric records into court due to the alleged confessions. The general goal was to paint Kevin's stay in the psychiatric facility as "warehousing" rather than treatment, arguing he was put there to keep him away from the police. Patients would argue that Kevin was treated differently, allowed to do different things, not participate in group therapy, and seemingly not given medication. Even Mayor Stephen Alfred would state that there was "concern" from citizens that Kevin was "on the loose." Kevin was reported to have openly wept in the courtroom when hearing these accusations at pre-trial hearings. It was eventually ruled by Sweeney that Kevin's psychiatric records would be inadmissible at the trial.

CHAPTER 7 : ONE DAUGHTER, TWO SONS

The aggravated murder trial of Kevin Young for the death of Lisa Lee Pruett would begin on June 28, 1993, with jurors and alternates sworn in. Carmen Marino and co-prosecutor Karl Wetzel would attempt to paint Kevin as a demented, woman-hating time bomb who killed Lisa out of jealous rage. However, Marino and Wetzel would also have to act as defense counsel of sorts to another young man whom defense attorney Mark DeVan and co-counsel J. Michael Murray would go after hard as the real killer, Lisa's boyfriend Daniel Dreifort. Two teenage sons, each vouched for by parents as being inside their homes as Lisa was stabbed to death around 12:30 a.m. that September night. The Cleveland and national media would both be paying close attention, as the early version of Court TV covered the trial nationally, though not carried by all cable providers.

Marino would open that Dan Dreifort had been cleared by Shaker Heights authorities two years prior. An FBI profile of the killing indicated a "very demented mentality" in the killer and stated the body was displayed to make it appear as sexual assault to throw authorities off the right track. DeVan would bring up the fact that twelve empty cough syrup bottles were found in the search of Dan's room. Marino would argue that such a rage-filled murder would have to have a motive.

Classmates and friends were called to the stand to testify as to statements Kevin allegedly made in the past. Daniel Messinger would testify that Kevin said he hated Lisa and Dan Dreifort and wanted to kill them. Messinger would later admit that he didn't take the threats seriously, thinking, "There goes Kevin." Then it was time for Marino to preemptively put Dan Dreifort on the stand to begin defending the accusations against the now college student who was Lisa's boyfriend. On the stand, Dan would deny that cough syrup made him violent. DeVan would put the twelve empty bottles in front of him. It would be alluded to that Dan was a "collector" and kept many things around such as bottles and cans. Marino stated that the defense's theory—that Dreifort murdered Lisa in a Robitussin-induced frenzy—remained far from proven.

Robert Dreifort would take the stand to vouch for his son's alibi. He was the former administrator for the Cleveland Clinic Center for Children and Youth, no longer employed by the hospital system. Robert would testify that his son was placed in the psychiatric facility at the Cleveland Clinic for "adolescent adjustment problems." He further denied that substance abuse, specifically the cough syrup, was the reason for the placement and it was made in consultation with physicians.

Responding Officer Ed Curtin would testify on the stand that Dan Dreifort displayed clear eyes and speech with good eye contact that night on the scene. Curtin recalled Daniel being "nervous," having a "concerned attitude," and "scared" about what was going on. Curtin testified that he did not suspect Daniel of anything.

Deputy Coroner Robert Challener would testify to the autopsy findings. According to him, Lisa was stabbed nineteen times with a small pocketknife. Challener would characterize what he saw as an "eruption of violence."

Three former psychiatric patients plus a worker in the Laurelwood facility testified to statements Kevin allegedly made at the facility. Edythe Heinz would repeat her assertions that Kevin was treated differently and was never in group therapy. She testified that when she asked Kevin if he killed Lisa, "without hesitation, he said yes." DeVan questioned why she waited two years to make this assertion to the police. A Shaker Heights detective was called to explain three items photographed at the scene that were not in evidence. Anastasia Tressler, an assistant at Laurelwood, would testify to incriminating statements made by Kevin, but when DeVan requested her notes, they could not specifically be found.

Kevin's parents would be called to the stand for his defense. His mother, Maryanne, would testify to his phone call home after twenty hours of police interrogation and tests while he was in Columbus for college. She testified that he felt suicidal, and they placed him in Laurelwood for three months. Kevin's father, Tal, testified that Kevin was home with him playing video games and watching television at the time of the murder. The prosecution and defense were drawing to a close, with their all-important closing arguments crucial to making the case to the jury in this circumstantial case.

Carmen Marino would state emphatically that Daniel Dreifort would never be charged, that it was "not the way we do things." He went on that the theory of Daniel as the murder was a "great choice" for the defense, but a "stupid scenario." He furthered that Kevin was the only "true" suspect in the case for almost three years with "not one piece of evidence to contradict that."

Mark DeVan would counter that Daniel Dreifort had "a sick, sick mind." DeVan theorized that Daniel was high on cough syrup and engaging in consensual sex with Lisa on the lawn when things got out of control. Daniel "only had to run one hundred feet" to the safety of his house, opined the attorney. DeVan wanted to make a clear point to the jury that Daniel had never returned to the courtroom after his testimony. "He is ashamed because he knows more about this than he is saying," ended DeVan.

After three weeks of testimony, the jury retired to deliberate Kevin's guilt on July 19, 1993. After a bit more than ten hours of deliberation over two days, they returned their verdict on July 21. At around 4:30 that afternoon, the jury's verdict was read aloud to the courtroom: on the sole count of the aggravated murder of Lisa Lee Pruett, Kevin Young was found not guilty. One single handclap and a gasp were reported after the verdict was read. Emotionally, Kevin hugged his attorneys.

CHAPTER 8 : AFTERMATH AND THE UNENDING

After Kevin's verdict of *not guilty*, the media frenzy continued. The Pruetts released a statement that "it is clear to us that no one will be called to account for Lisa's murder." Immediate comments to the press were that Daniel Dreifort was an "easy target" for his abuse of cough syrup and a "one month stay for incorrigible behavior." The *Plain Dealer* further published that Daniel and Robert Dreifort passed lie detector tests. In the following week, an article titled "PUBLIC OPINION STILL CONDEMNS KEVIN YOUNG" stated that Daniel Dreifort had "passed a polygraph with flying colors."

Little more than a week after the verdict, the *Plain Dealer* published an article which included interviews of the jury foreperson and other details. It was reported that Kevin had flunked three lie detector tests and passed one. A story that he had drowned the family cat as a youth was thrown in, which was later disputed by family. Foreperson Nancy McMurtrey related that the notion Dan Dreifort had been driven to homicidal rage by cough syrup was laughed at. She opined that Carmen Marino was "great" but his story was also a stretch that didn't hold water. The paper alluded to ominous writings kept from the jury by a technicality in a search warrant. The defense had "blamed the whole mess on a conspiracy by police, whom they portrayed as bumbling Nazis."

McMurtrey furthered that the jury doubted the testimony of the Laurelwood patients. It didn't make sense to them. They wondered where Kenny Workman was and what testimony he could have added. "Nobody bought" that Daniel Dreifort could have been a suspect. "If cough medicine could cause people to commit murder, they wouldn't sell it over the counter, and you'd see empty bottles scattered all over downtown.

"It showed how weak the evidence was" McMurtrey went on, "as remote as saying Kevin Young did it." It seemed the jury had been presented a dueling preposterousness. The first jury vote was reported to be eight not guilty, three guilty, and one uncertain. The second vote went to ten to two, favoring acquittal; the third moving to eleven to one. Finally, the last holdout agreed. McMurtrey related that the group did not want to hand off the responsibility to another jury.

That same article reported other concerning things. It stated that an anonymous letter to local radio station WWWE alleged that the majority of the jury believed that Kevin was the killer. A quote from Dr. Philip Resnik was published that "there's something in there" in reference to Kevin's psychiatric records. "I saw it. Oh, there's something there," he added.

On August 1, 1993, the date of that *Plain Dealer* article, police were called to the Ridgebury Boulevard bridge which overpassed Interstate 271, the busiest suburban freeway for the eastern suburbs of Cleveland. A young man climbed out on to the rail, apparently preparing to jump into the highway traffic below. Police stopped traffic on the busy highway below for fifteen minutes. Sergeant Cliff Uzell of the Mayfield Heights Police spoke in a fatherly way to the despondent young man, eventually talking him off the edge. It was Kevin. He had been distraught from the *Plain Dealer* story. DeVan was "furious" at the irresponsible journalism.

The *Plain Dealer* and others didn't stop there. On September 14, 2002, they published that Kevin was to appear in court on menacing charges. The date being the twelfth anniversary of Lisa's death hardly seems coincidental. Over the past three to four weeks, parents had been calling SHPD and the media expressing fear of Kevin working in the area as a painter. An anonymous mother stated, "A lot of young girls live around here and we're afraid that Kevin Young is a time bomb just waiting to go off." No matter what a jury would decide, Kevin's life was irreparably altered by whatever happened that one September night. He would descend into substance abuse. He would be found dead in his Cleveland Heights apartment on January 14, 2017, at the age of forty-four.

CHAPTER 9 : THE FRANKENSTEIN SHOES

After my first reading of *Little, Crazy Children*, I was left with suspicions, but certainly not anything anyone else hadn't thought of over the years. I sent Renner an email telling him I enjoyed the book and thought he had done a good job with it. I left him with the quandy: "if the polygraph had never been invented, does the boyfriend go on trial instead of Kevin?" Renner had explicitly written that a prosecutor could have made a case against Daniel Dreifort that stood a chance of having a jury convict him, and I agreed with that assertion. It would have been a far-from-perfect case, a difficult one, but there would be people on a jury who could have made that conclusion. Maybe the case just needed one thing to point to.

Whenever I read or watch any kind of true crime case, I look at it through my training and experience as a small-city police officer. I could definitely imagine the stress of trying to handle an outdoor homicide scene in the middle of the night and all the things involved. There were so many things to do, places to look, and there was still the rest of a city that could need a service call at any time. I have the advantage of looking at everything in hindsight and choosing what to concentrate on and what to ignore. Those officers, any police officers on a scene, typically do not. For a stabbing death, any good police officer will be searching for a weapon, blood where it should not be, and in this case, a pair of shoes which might match any important footwear evidence. Those were the fundamentals.

It was written in Renner's book that a footwear impression made in blood was recovered at the scene and that a "herringbone" pattern was displayed in the impression. Many kinds of impressions can be important to investigators looking into different crimes and occurrences. Fingerprints and footprints are definitely important clues, but can often be innocently left. If your footprint is found in your yard, or your fingerprints or DNA are found on something that is perfectly reasonable for you to have contacted, it can mean nothing and is a normal occurrence. If an impression is made in a victim's blood at a crime scene, that has to mean that an object came into contact with that blood after the victim bled out, and it becomes an exceptionally important piece of evidence as it puts a relative timestamp and location on that object's impression. That footwear impression would have to mean that a pair of shoes stepped in the victim's blood after her stabbing, in a location where her blood would have been, presumably close to her or her previous position after being stabbed.

Whoever had stabbed Lisa would have some amount of blood on their person, likely their hands and the weapon. It would not have to be reminiscent of a horror movie scene—blood can take time to exit, or remain contained inside the victim's body. It could have been a small to moderate amount, but *some* amount would be on the assailant. The prologue of *Little, Crazy Children*, confirmed by actual statements in files, details Daniel Dreifort's initial police interview inside the Shaker Heights Police Station. He was asked to describe his clothing and footwear. He lists a t-shirt, bathing trunks, and that he had worn his Converse Chuck Taylor All-Star high-top sneakers with a tie-dyed color pattern the previous evening.

To me, as an investigator, the most suspicious thing I read in the book was that Daniel had been interviewed wearing a pair of bathing trunks. It's not unbelievable that a teenager could have thrown on a pair of trunks for lounging around the house. This might be more applicable to men than women; I would think a woman wouldn't lounge around in a one-piece swimsuit or bikini unless sunbathing in the yard. I know I have thrown on a pair of swim trunks for just lounging around, but I wouldn't have worn them out and about the whole day as back in the day, they were usually made without any pockets for the things a person would typically want to take with them. There was no mention in the book or in statements of a pool or trip to the beach—it was mid-September with school in session, though weather records list the high temperature on September 13, 1990, as eighty degrees. I found it highly unlikely that someone would have worn swim trunks that entire day, and it was my suspicion that Daniel changed his clothes.

The second most suspicious thing I read was father Robert Dreifort's official statement to police. In it, he seems to overly, and unnaturally, account for his son's clothing and footwear as seen inside the house. He additionally adds that he had been naked before exiting the house. I wondered if a father was covering up the actions of his son. All of this was just suspicion and speculation. What would it prove to someone? Just suspicion at best, no?

That blood impression was the key—something tangible and impossible to dispute—or so I believed. Well, I had a start with the statement of a likely suspect listing the shoes he was wearing at the time. On a break, I sat down at a shared computer and looked up Converse Chuck Taylor All-Stars. I couldn't remember ever wearing a pair of these shoes; there might be an old picture or two of me as a toddler with some, but I didn't remember ever wearing or picking out a pair of these at a store. Chuck Taylor All-Star shoes have literally been made for over a century; generations have worn these common shoes, having never gone out of style. The enduring version can be traced back to the 1930s. I started looking all over the internet for the sole patterns, and they all seemed to have very standard soles, which did not appear relevant to the case. There were modern versions with higher heels for the ladies, but those weren't relevant either. The brown rubber soles seemed standard. It was a strikeout.

A momentary letdown led me to force myself to ask a question, if for nothing else to be thorough. Could the specific model have been made differently at a certain time? I had simply done one Google search. Why not do another one? I entered the terms "1980s Chuck Taylor All Star tie-dyed" into Google. Up popped an array of sales ads for different examples of the shoes, most with the "psychedelic" tie-dye patterns. I looked at all of them on the screen, but one soon stood out. It was an Etsy ad for a beat-up pair of Chucks supposedly from the 1980s. What drew my eye to this ad was that there was an extra heel portion of both shoes that did not match the color or the tread pattern of the rest of the sole. This extra heel was white, as opposed to the rest of the brown rubber sole, and seemed to be between one-quarter and one-third of an inch in height, similar to a heel on a men's dress shoe. It was a Frankenstein of a shoe; not in the sense that Boris Karloff or someone at a Halloween party would wear it, but it seemed to be a part of a totally different shoe attached to a pair of the most common shoes made in modern times. The tread pattern on this extra heel was a repeating zig-zag lines. I double checked every definition and example of the term "herringbone" I could find on the internet and it seemed like it could match.

There it was—quite possibly the key to solving the murder of Lisa Pruett—sitting on a computer screen in a sales ad.

There I was, staring at an image of something on a computer screen, something that should have been discarded decades ago, residing now in a landfill. It was something I could not ignore.

CHAPTER 10 : THE MAGNIFYING GLASS

I had to email Renner. If there was a simple way to establish who killed Lisa, it was in linking the Frankenstein shoe to that blood impression written about in the book. But there was something else that would have had to be true. The obvious implication became that the police on scene that night never seized or examined Dan Dreifort's shoes. I asked Renner in an email if he had any copies of a picture of the blood impression and any evidence lists or supplemental police reports from the scene listing evidence taken from the house or outdoor scene.

I got a response from Renner that seemed to allude he didn't have time or desire to dig through his acquired files from the case, but he gladly shared a cache of photos. Renner was likely busy on other things, and his book clearly stated that some of the files he had acquired had been destroyed in a flood years earlier. I opened the files, and found four labeled sections: CRIME SCENE, DAN ROOM, KEVIN HOUSE, and KEVIN DORM.

My first realization from browsing all four sections was there had to have been a lot more pictures taken at that homicide scene than was in Renner's cache. First off, there were no pictures of the victim's body, which did not surprise me. Our victim was a child, a juvenile female left exposed. Photos of a juvenile victim exposed, if taken at all, could be construed as illegal images, child pornography, and I did not expect them to be distributed. What I cannot tell you, reader, is that I have any knowledge on any typical policies or practices regarding photography or photographs regarding juvenile victims. There were many pictures of Lisa's bicycle propped up against the bushy vegetation along the Lee Road sidewalk. The DAN ROOM section seemed to be all taken indoors, as well as the less extensive KEVIN HOUSE and KEVIN DORM sections. Running through the KEVIN HOUSE and KEVIN DORM sections revealed nothing, just glaring normalcy. All the files consisted of digital images taken of between one and four old 35mm film prints or Polaroid instants.

My memories of my friend Gene drifted to the times I recalled him looking at pictures. He would suddenly have a magnifying glass up to the picture, like the good detective he must have been. I laugh because I had no idea where on his person he procured this magnifier from. Gene was old school, probably one of the last, if not the last, police officers to carry a blackjack on his duty belt until it was suggested he no longer carry the weapon. He taught a community college class on criminal investigation. One of the local officers told me he had taken Gene's class and their project was to stage a crime scene at home, take pictures, take measurements, and draw a diagram. He went on to tell me how he had "killed" his wife in his living room rather extravagantly. Gene returned his project with comments that he did a good job, but with comedic remarks about the sweater he was wearing in a family picture on the wall. That was Gene.

If there were any details in those pictures Renner shared, I would have to channel Gene a bit, and luckily, instead of a Sherlock Holmes-sized glass, the computer offered a small magnifying glass icon to click on until it would click no more. CRIME SCENE consisted of only twenty-two prints, all taken outdoors. Quite a number of pictures of the sidewalk and Lisa's bicycle leaned against the brush. There were two pictures of a patio with black chairs and a pair of shoes left outside against the brick wall of the house. An additional photo showed an investigator holding the shoes up to photograph their soles. Two pictures showed an old hammer on the ground alongside the house. The hammer didn't seem to be relevant to the case.

The first picture that really drew my attention was that of a clear plastic bag laying on the ground. It seemed to contain a small paper item inside, and there seemed to be two small, rusty-brown-to-red areas on the upper surface that seemed to have been left by someone tracking something on it. It seemed consistent with the type of plastic bag a newspaper deliverer would put their paper in to throw it into a yard or driveway. It seemed to be the subject of the photo but it was not taken close enough or at the right angle to determine if there was a footwear pattern in those rusty brown areas. Could this have been the bag I was looking for? Renner's book listed a herringbone-patterned impression in blood found on a paper bag with a periodical inside it. This was clearly not a paper bag, and it puzzled me. The clear bag in the picture also appeared to be partially on top of something white on the ground. I would later conclude, though not at that moment, that the white thing had to be a plaster footprint casting being made on the ground. Why would the bag be on top of this?

I moved to the DAN ROOM folder of pictures, which contained digital images of forty-one old 35mm prints taken indoors. The first picture that drew my attention was a plastic grocery-style bag containing a brown paper bag, which then contained at least two boxes and bottles which corresponded to generic brands of cough syrup. Other pictures placed the bag in what clearly seems like the bedroom of a messy teenage boy. This brought the issue of

Robo parties and the effects of overdosing on cough syrup to mind. Renner's book detailed a cross-examination between defense attorney Mark DeVan and Dan Dreifort in which DeVan tripped Dan up on the question of the recency of the purchase of these quantities of cough syrup in relation to the murder. DeVan illustrated how the lot numbers on the boxes pointed to purchases made very close to that day, which he hoped would illustrate Dan's desire for a Robo party that fateful night. A print in the same digital image showed a pocketknife in a wooden bin, and Renner's book said that the pocketknife was seized to be analyzed by the coroner's office. So these pictures display two items which had to be seized from inside the Dreifort residence.

Scanning around the pictures taken inside a bedroom put many things in view. There is a small bed, a small couch, posters, a bottle and can collection, and a shoebox collection, amongst other things. Looking at the bed, there were two pillows with white pillowcases, a blanket on top, and nothing covering a bare mattress. I found it strange, but there was also some kind of small couch or futon in the room which could serve as a sleeping space. There were some pictures taken in at least one different room. One showed a hand pointing to a piece of paper. I have no idea how the item pointed to could be in the least related to the case.

Then there they were—a digital image of three 35mm prints of a pair of shoes on a wooden floor near a corner of a hallway wall and what appeared to be a metal stand of a wooden musical instrument. There was a rug nearby and what appeared to be the landing of a staircase. The shoes were clearly a pair of Converse Chuck Taylor All-Star high tops. The famous Chuck Taylor All-Star circular logo is visible on the left shoe's inner ankle section. This was definitely something I had been looking for. The three pictures were very similar, all taken from what seemed to be close to eye level of a photographer at a downward angle. Were they made the same as the Frankenstein shoes? I only had photos at a horrible angle to try to determine that. I clicked the magnifier as far as it would go and tried to study the heels of these shoes to link it to the blood impression. Only the slightest sliver of one of the shoe's heel portion was barely visible at an angle. I pored over these three pictures for quite a while on the computer screen, looking for that one thing that would determine if these shoes in the pictures had the Frankenstein heels. It was just such a horrible angle to try to make any determination, and after many minutes, I gave up. I closed out the files and left it alone for that day.

The next evening, I couldn't let it go; I had to give it another shot to see what those pictures said. I opened up the files again and began to magnify and pore over the rear section of that one shoe on that wooden floor. I studied and studied the pictures, trying to view it from every angle. I went back to the pictures of the Frankenstein shoes online to try to match one detail, figure out one thing to determine if those were the shoes on the wooden floor. How would those extra heels look at that angle? Would it smooth out, or would a corner jut out to prove it had to be those extra heels? The middle picture of the three similar shots was slightly different. I spent more time on that print, the tapering image of the rear of the right shoe looked a little different in that print. It seemed to possibly jut out a little bit from the rest of the profile of the sole, but the image started to blur the heel section at that magnification. I kept at it to find that one thing; that one thing had to be there. The two other pictures showed a more gradual sole profile, the middle one's right heel almost started to blur into the floor where the Frankenstein heel would start. I kept going over and over it until I had to stop myself and conclude that I could neither identify that these shoes had special heels nor exclude the possibility that they did. I had given it my best and had to give up and admit where the photo evidence was. Little did I realize giving up on the heel of those shoes would free me.

My eyes and focus relaxed a bit, and my gaze began to back away, pan out a bit. There was a dark spot evident on the right shoe's white rubber toecap in all three pictures. I hadn't paid much attention to it until giving up on the heels. That middle picture I had concentrated on and left my gaze on began to tell a story. The dark spot on that white rubber toecap in this print showed a bright, deep pink edge to it, and a mostly rusty brown body. My eyes flared at what I had overlooked for many, many minutes in analyzing the heels of the shoes with a laser focus. For all future purposes in this book, I will refer to this spot in this crime scene photo as potential blood evidence. I knew from hunting and fishing that blood can come in many different shades and colors from wherever it bled from the body of an animal. How could I have overlooked that? The pictures' eye-level viewpoints certainly didn't immediately lead me to any conclusions about the spots. Could it have been easily overlooked by the photographer at that distance as well? So many things started to race into my mind. It could have all been a mistake, human error.

I emailed Renner and told him what I thought I found in the pictures. I told him I needed to see the files, the police reports. He suggested I take it to the Shaker Heights Police. I couldn't argue against that being the right thing to do. This picture alone could have constituted exculpatory evidence with respect to the accusation of Kevin Young in Lisa's murder. It should have prevented his trial.

CHAPTER 11 : THE WALK-IN

I couldn't sleep, no matter how much I wanted to since I had to work in the evening. I planned to go down to the station the following day, but I couldn't sleep because this couldn't wait. I went to the library to type up my report, just a page and three quarters. I had put more effort and done longer reports on DUI arrests, and that bothered me. I had the printouts of photos I wanted and made them into two packets containing the report and pictures, in case I needed to leave them at the desk or just simply shove them into someone's hands. I felt ready. I put the copies inside the pages of my *Little, Crazy Children*, which was marked with cut-up Post-It notes indicating the important parts. I headed out the door. How many people have the finest moments of their career twenty years after they walked away from it?

Shaker Heights PD was listed on Lee Road, so I figured once I got myself to Lee, I could find it. I was familiar with South Woodland, so I got off the freeway and found the road which would eventually get me to Lee. Familiarity wasn't the only reason. When I finally got to the Lee Road intersection, I slowly made the right turn to view the scene—the point on Earth where Lisa Lee Pruett was found thirty-three years earlier, and whose cause I was about to advance. The spot looked much different, no real bushes anymore as seen in photos. As I drove out of view, I realized by the crossing roads and addresses that I had needed to turn left on Lee instead of right, so I detoured and returned southbound past the former Dreifort house and backyard where a young light was extinguished. I needed to see it.

I walked into the Shaker Heights Police Station/Municipal Court Complex and went to the police window. An elderly clerk on a mobility scooter came to the window, and I explained I had information on a crime and requested to speak with a detective. He asked what kind of crime. His eyebrows shot up and jaw opened when I told him murder. He asked if it was recent, and I told him it was an old case. He asked me to wait as he motored back into a hallway. He returned and told me someone would be with me. I sat on a bench. I figured someone was probably preparing an interview room and I would probably be recorded.

After a few minutes, a side door opened and a tall, African American detective came out dressed in a shirt and tie, introduced himself, and shook my hand.

I introduced myself and immediately told him, "I'm a former police officer. I'm not here to waste your time." I needed that to build a little bit of opening credibility. No officer knows who you are and has to figure you out—if you're a crank, idiot, whatever. He led me inside to a small interview room with a small desk. I knew which seat to sit in. He got my basic information and asked where I was a police officer. We talked and I found out he had started in the early 1990s, just a year or so after Lisa's murder. Damn, I had hoped to find someone without a connection to the original investigation, and I got the senior detective who had worked well past retirement age, into his fifties. He was handsome and in good shape though. He wanted to know if I had any connections to Shaker Heights, any connection to any of the people, figures in the case. I told him I wasn't sure as this was more than the second time I had ever been in the city; I knew I had gone to an estate sale there in my picker phase.

I wanted to quickly move to my findings, so I showed him the book. He said he thought he remembered Renner coming around in the past few years, but had not read the book. I didn't know if he had ever personally worked the case, so I summarized how Lisa was found stabbed to death outside in the adjacent yard to her boyfriend's house. I then told how I read that there was a footwear impression in blood left on a bag at the scene and how that would be possibly the most important piece of physical evidence. I brought out pictures of the Frankenstein shoes advertised on Etsy, and explained that I had done Google searches on what model of shoes the book listed that Daniel Dreifort stated he was wearing the previous evening. "If you're wearing something in 1990, it was probably manufactured in the 1980s. I put '1980s Chuck Taylor tie-dye' into Google and one example of this came up." These heels could possibly make the pattern described in the book made in blood as "herringbone."

He took it in as I moved to pictures of Daniel's bedroom. I told him I would have thought his mother would have a bed made and ready because he was coming home from the hospital that very day. His bed showed two pillows with white cases and a blanket, but nothing covering a bare mattress. I speculated that whoever killed Lisa would have some blood on him, and a teen would likely return to his room, so there could have been blood transfer onto the sheets or they could have been used to conceal bloody clothing in laundry. I then moved to the images of the clear plastic bag on the ground with possible blood tracks outside the Dreifort house. I noted that those possible tracks were small enough to be left by just the heel of a shoe. He had been following along. I knew he was trying to figure out me as well as what I was showing him. I then produced the black-and-white image of three old 35mm prints of Chuck Taylor All-Star high-top shoes on a wooden floor. I told him these matched what Daniel stated he was wearing the night of the murder, and I couldn't get a good look at what kind of heel was on the shoe to determine if it was a Frankenstein shoe because the angle the photos were taken from.

"Let me show you what this middle picture shows when you blow it up."

I pulled out my smartphone and located the thumbnail for the magnified pics. I pressed on the first of the two levels of magnification I wanted to show him when I noticed he moved closer to my personal space and leaned into me, as an interrogator can do at times. I scrolled between the two pictures—one showing the total of the shoes magnified, the second just the front end of the shoes. I didn't need to say a word. I looked up to the most serious intensity possible in a human face.

"And presumably that's blood!"

The entire tenor of the person and the interview immediately changed. I could tell he was moved, shaken by what I had shown him. I tried to imagine the things going on in his mind. He took my little two-page report and hunched over to read it carefully and intensely. He muttered that they had taken another look at the case five to six years prior and found nothing. Shortly after he mentioned that, his former coworker (who had worked on the case recently) told him that he was still sure they had the right suspect in Kevin. I wish I had asked the name of that coworker, but I didn't care in the moment. I was trying to hand this football off and not insert myself into another organization's investigation.

He began to ask confirmation questions, multiple times, where I had gotten these pictures. I repeatedly answered that I had gotten them from Renner. I told him I assumed Renner got them from Freedom of Information Act (FOIA) requests at some point, either from the prosecutor's office or from SHPD. I told him I didn't have any idea what would have been sent to the prosecutor for trial and what would be kept back at the department. He tried to search for an ulterior motive from me, and I told him I was just trying to help and be a good citizen. The man was stunned and shaken; things he held in belief for decades had likely come crashing down. I was sure I could imagine most of the things going on in his head, but I didn't know the whole truth at the time. He circled around on questions many times, wanting to know everything about me and where I had gotten these pictures. I had told him about first learning about it at a library presentation. He asked me about where I had met Renner. Circling to see if I gave any inconsistent responses.

"Well, Renner came to my library three weeks ago."

"You've had this book for three weeks?" Unintentional compliments can often be the most sincere. "So you believe this would lead to a successful prosecution?"

"Yes, I do."

It may have been a question to establish a certain criteria to reopen the case to supervisors or department policy. He confirmed my contact info and I answered affirmatively that he could contact me if he needed to. It had only been between fifteen and twenty minutes, and I got up to leave. I offered him my book, but he didn't need it. As I was disappearing out the door to the lobby, I heard the old senior detective yell, "You have a good Christmas now!" I had earned his respect in those fifteen minutes, maybe his admiration.

I returned home and went to sleep. I knew that he now knew. I knew that he knew that I knew. I knew that he knew that I knew that he knew. But I had so much more to learn. I only had some pictures. I emailed Renner and he thanked me.

CHAPTER 12 : WALLS OF THOUGHT

Justice takes time, so I moved my focus away from the case and tried not to think about it for at least a couple months. Cases had to be built, prosecutors consulted, and a presentation to a grand jury had to be orchestrated. None of these things would be accomplished in days or a few weeks. But there were a few obvious things about the case that bothered me a great deal. This had to be a colossal and catastrophic case of human error in a major case of the murder of a young girl. I worried the city might slow roll or ignore the case out of sheer embarrassment. Having your police department be so wrong on a high-profile case was going to be a huge hit to the city's image, and my brief time in suburban law enforcement taught me that image can often trump other interests. Reputations matter to officials; careers are thought of over many interests too.

I thought back to the senior detective and our brief time in that interview room. I tried to think of what was going through his mind as I showed him the things I had found. Walls of thought had to be crashing down as something he was led to believe for an entire career had been shown they could not now be truc. Idcas and faith in people had to be immediately questioned. Little did I know the walls of thought of another important figure in the case would become frustrating impediments to me. At some point, I would have a reckoning with my own walls.

I was both a former police officer and a private citizen, and had to figure out what role and responsibility I had as both. I clearly wanted to help further the case in any way I could without inserting myself into the case. I thought I was handing off a football in a crucial game with a clear path to the end zone. I didn't want to interfere or do things which could turn people off. But I was also a private citizen who didn't have a career or reputation to worry about. I had no boss to tell me what to do or what not to do. I held a strong belief that there were things owed to the families involved if the authorities did nothing with what I had taken them. What limits I should set became a question for me. I told myself that if no actions were taken within a year of when I showed the Shaker Heights Police the evidence I found, I would offer the same evidence to the Pruetts and the Youngs. They deserved the truth for what had happened and what they went through. Another thought that formed in my mind was that if I hadn't seen any news in the case in six months, I would start to worry. There would be some, but it had quite the opposite effect.

Near the end of February, my curiosity came back to me and I went to Google to look for anything new on the case, and I was in for quite a shock. The search popped up with a FOX8.com news story dated February 6, titled, "A FRESH LOOK AT DECADES-OLD MURDERS IN SHAKER HEIGHTS" by Dave Nethers, in which he interviewed James Renner about the case. After giving the backstories of Lisa's murder and the murders of Cleveland *Plain Dealer* editor Philip Porter and his wife Dorothy, the story went on to print, "He has written about his conclusions in a book called *Little, Crazy Children*, and on Monday was invited to the Shaker Heights Police Department to share those conclusions with investigators more than three decades after the murders."

The story went on to Renner stating that the meeting went very well and how he believed there could be answers very soon. The very next stanza continued the reckless assertion at the end of the book that the actual killer of all three persons was a different person (David Branagan), who also was deceased.

My mind was in a fog of confusion after reading about the actions of both Shaker Heights Police and Renner. I had clued him in on the blood spot and my presentation to Shaker Heights months earlier. Why would he continue to publicly support the Branagan theory on the same amount of evidence as there was against Kevin Young? Why in the world would Shaker Heights want to hear Renner's ideas after I had taken them enough evidence for indictments of the Dreiforts? I felt mystified and betrayed by both. My first inclination was that it was some sort of public relations move on Shaker Heights' part, or some kind of fact-finding mission to find out how much Renner actually knew. They already knew what I knew. What had really happened in that meeting? I had to get back into things.

I again looked up what I thought was the missing link, the key evidence that started leading to the truth of Lisa's murder—the Frankenstein shoes. Once again, Google led me straight to the ad for the sale of the shoes. It was months later and they still were on sale, which didn't surprise me as they were a beat-up thirty-five-year-old pair of junk sneakers someone was foolishly hoping to get ninety dollars for. It bothered me that Shaker Heights had not purchased them.

I contacted the seller for the shoes in order to ask questions. I asked if they were the owner of the shoes, and if not, how they determined the shoes were from the 1980s. The seller replied that the location of a trademark symbol on the logo on the shoe's insole meant it was from the 1980s. Later on, the niche website, the Chucks Connection, dedicated to this line of shoes, confirmed this assertion. I searched around, emailed the niche website, and could not find any other example or confirmation of this rare model of the shoe. It was time; I could not let this lone example which may lead to Lisa Pruett's truth be lost to the shuffle of time. The Frankenstein shoes were marked down to seventy-five bucks, and the right fool was found to pay a total of ninety-nine dollars for the thirty-five-year-old, worn down, piece-of-crap pair of Chucks. I did feel like a fool, but they were in my possession, and that would be important.

I reached out to Renner and began to search the Shaker Heights Police website when I found the next fact that shocked me to the core. In searching the police website for a directory of officers or detectives, I clicked on the link listed for the Investigations Bureau and was taken to the biography page of the administrator in charge of the Bureau, Commander Timothy Kohanski. A wave went through my body as I realized the name could not be a coincidence, and went on to read that Timothy was the son of long-time Shaker Heights Detective Thomas Kohanski. The elder Kohanski was tasked with the polygraph examinations and community relations in the original investigation of Lisa's murder. The polygraphs had to be wrong, at least misleading, though inadmissible in court. The information given to community leaders about Kevin was inaccurate. This was a mountain of a conflict of interest to be in charge of a new investigation that your own father was a big part of.

I emailed Renner asking about the meeting and what was discussed. He relayed that he realized during the meeting that Timothy was the son of Tom Kohanski, and that he was very nice. Renner furthered that an eager young detective was being placed in charge of the case of all three murders and he believed they were taking it seriously. I then asked for the name of that detective and informed him I had purchased the shoes in question that started to solve the case. He never replied back. Whether he deserved it or not, this was the moment I decided not to trust James Renner on this case anymore. He was still the biggest hero of the case to me, but I didn't know where his head was anymore.

I went on to find more things on the internet that bothered and disturbed me about the case. Following some social media and Reddit threads, I found a reply from Renner to a questioner that the case had to be taken out of the hands of SHPD. Later, Renner's 2015 *Cleveland Scene* article, "Northeast Ohio's 50 Most Frustrating Cold Cases," listed Lisa's death as number five. The thing that stood out the most is that Renner listed where to call in tips for every case, and that for Lisa's case he listed the Cuyahoga County Sheriff's Office. Renner clearly distrusted the Shaker Heights Police Department in the years before writing *Little, Crazy Children*, then went on to give them a presentation and change his mind.

Maybe the most important thing I found scouring the internet was something that I could not find for many months of poking my nose in this case. Following things that kept popping up on Google searches that spring, I found a tiny image of what looked like a black-and-white picture of plaster footwear castings. I clicked on the image, which led me to a Renner post on an obscure blog called *Tapatalk*. Renner posted an image of four plaster footwear castings and asked the blog if anyone could identify the shoes that would have made any of these impressions in regards to Lisa's case. I was stunned. Nowhere in his book or any of the things I had read were there any mentions of footwear castings being taken. That had to mean that the police had to be paying attention to footwear evidence on that first day of the investigation. It was the point which made me realize that the clear plastic bag on the ground with potential blood tracks on it was on top of a setting cast of footwear impressions.

I scanned the photographs of the casts and they appeared to be collections of Impressions rather than just one cast each of one full footwear impression. This made sense to me in that they were likely taken in high-traffic areas, and full impressions can be hard to make and leave, depending on the hardness of the soil in question. The Frankenstein shoes I had bought had the zig-zag herringbone heel with three wave crest/wave bottom patterns across their breadth, then the shoe's sole transitioned to the traditional Chuck Taylor All-Star sole with straight diagonal lines. There was one cast where a partial impression seemed to show a three wave crest/wave bottom pattern across the breadth of it, then some diagonal lines above it. I found this partial impression consistent with the old Frankenstein shoes I had purchased. This did not in any way prove anything with regard to the commission of the murder. What it did support, however, was that there was a model of the shoes with Frankenstein heels in the area to have made that impression. A link to the blood impression listed in the book would have gone towards proving the murder.

I went back to those first pictures of the Chuck Taylor All-Stars I had seen to see if yet another look could shed any more light, and it amazingly delivered just that. Looking closely at the most magnified versions of the shoes I could manage, a much more subtle clue began to become apparent. Looking at the white rubber front portions of both shoes, a pink haze started to show on many areas of the white rubber of both shoes. It looked like a residue, something drying up or congealing on both shoes, and there was some possible dark pink staining on the canvas of the right shoe. What was a pink substance that could be relevant to the facts of this case as was reported? It had to be cough syrup. The residue all over both shoes corresponded to some kind of cough syrup being spilled or splashed somehow on both shoes. This seemed to batter down the assertion of Daniel Dreifort that he was not planning or engaging in Robo that night.

Having all the thoughts of this chapter rattling around in my head, I went back to the three pictures of the Chuck Taylors on that wooden floor. I had concentrated on one of the pictures more than the other two because there were slight differences in the photos, whereas at arm's length, one's first inclination is that they could be triplicate. They could not be triplicate due to the differences I had magnified and found. They had to be three individual photos, three separate clicks of a camera's shutter. *Do you take three pictures of something that you're not paying attention to?* The rhetorical question began to bother me.

There was a dark thought that came into my mind a couple times while thinking about those pictures and the case as a whole, and it came back to me and started to challenge my own wall of thought. The dark thought was that I could have attempted to extort people with those pictures. My efforts to that point had proved to me that the potential blood evidence was hard to see and had taken me some time to discover, even though I was thoroughly examining the pictures for the heel sections of the shoes. It had not hit me immediately—I had to spend time and effort with the pictures. Was my frame of mind hindering me? My wall of thought suddenly started to crumble one day, and I had to admit to myself there was a potential, a possibility that what I was seeing was not some kind of human error; it could have been deliberate. I started to curse at myself as it started to begin making sense of aspects of the case. I felt naïve, but more importantly, I began to think I may have placed myself in a precarious situation.

I needed help… from someone I could trust.

CHAPTER 13 : THE FBI AND ME PD

Law enforcement agencies help each other each and every day in this country. Local, state, and federal authorities can be assisting each other or collaborating in a wide range of ways at any given moment. It especially exists between neighboring jurisdictions and in small towns. I had been a small-city police officer, and I remembered another young officer in the area I had known and collaborated with who had moved on to another position in the justice system. I had run into him once in the interim years, and had even seen him on the news once. He was someone I knew—and knew I could trust. He also was in a position which very well could give me some good advice, maybe even help.

I tracked down an address and showed up at his residence and knocked on his door on a weekend. It had been at least fifteen years, so I had to reintroduce myself. He didn't have much time so I briefly told him I was possibly in a precarious situation. I quickly told him about reading the book and about the case of Lisa Pruett. I tried to give a quick synopsis of the case, pulling out one of my Frankenstein shoes, and showing him the crime scene pictures of the shoes in question on the wooden floor.

He took it all in calmly, then interjected, "Mike, I need to ask you why you're bringing this to me."

I went into how at first glance it looked to me like it was just a big mistake, an oversight, just human error. Then I had to tell him that my opinion was evolving due to a lot of other facts, such as the multiple pictures taken, other footwear evidence coming to light, and nothing was happening in the case. I stated this could easily have been a covered-up murder and it was starting to make more sense that it was. I told him I had no idea what to do, no idea if I was in a bad spot or not. I told him I needed whatever help or advice he could give me about the case. I had no idea what to do or who to go to. He looked at the pictures and took it seriously. He gave me his card and said he would contact some people and see what the best route was. I was extremely thankful to be heard and that I might have some help with the case.

I got back in contact with my old acquaintance and he told me he was trying to set up a meeting with a regional FBI agent for me to present the case to him. It would, at best, be a rag-tag presentation with no official documents and only some of the pictures. I had to give, as quickly as possible, a rundown of the case and how it essentially came down to two suspects—two young male classmates who had psychological issues and whose families both insisted they were inside their houses at the time of the murder. I drew copies of a crime scene sketch by hand since I had none. I had a printout that indicated the Shaker Heights Investigations Bureau was headed by Tim Kohanski, son of the detective who had done the polygraphs in the original investigation, and how there was a familial conflict of interest that could mean someone was being protected. I would have to try to get my theory of how the murder resulted from an involuntary haircutting fantasy, supported by a picture of clippers left outside on a porch. As I write this, I can imagine how disjointed and all over the place it would have seemed.

The biggest thing I wanted to convey was the strength of what that picture of the Chuck Taylor All-Stars showed. I wanted to tie in the fact that this was an outdoor crime. The crime scene, especially at night, would have required so much attention outdoors that the search and photography inside the Dreifort residence would have been conducted by a relatively small number of people. The people inside the Dreifort house would have been able to see this piece of evidence that all the people and officers outside scouring the yards and neighborhood would not have been privy to.

Within a couple of weeks, I sat down in a conference room with my old acquaintance and an agent from the FBI. I started into my rag-tag presentation with hand-drawn sketches and a rundown of my haircutting theory and the whittling of the case down to two suspects: Kevin Young and Dan Dreifort. I had printed out magnified views of those Chuck Taylors on the wooden floor. I went into what I had given the Shaker Heights detective and the things I had learned in the interim. I pulled out the Frankenstein shoes and a blown-up picture of the footwear cast, which I thought showed a promising match to the heel. I then went into how the person currently in charge of the Investigations Bureau's father had been an integral part of the original investigation through the polygraph examinations. The FBI agent had to start with the fact that a homicide is a local, state charge, and not something that the federal authorities could bring charges on. I insisted that there was a potential of something more. Someone or something looked like it was being protected.

"Mike, Tom Kohanski is dead," my acquaintance chimed in.

It was a detail I had not looked into. It didn't seem to change the fundamentals of what the case could be, at least not to me. They obviously had done some homework on the case prior to the meeting, which made sense to me.

The FBI agent asked, "Mike, don't you think this all could be just a mistake? I mean, we make mistakes, I make mistakes."

I agreed about mistakes; it had been my initial inclination. But I pressed that there were multiple pictures of the shoes taken as the focus of each picture; they were not in the background or side ground of the photo. I pressed that someone would not take pictures of something they weren't paying attention to.

"So what are you saying, that someone gave these guys, like, a hundred bucks?" the agent went on. It was a dismissive question with the idea that something like this would involve a petty amount. He was trying to dismiss the whole thing.

I couldn't investigate into anything that possibly was exchanged or agreed on, but I thought I had established enough cause to show that there was a distinct possibility that the photos showed there was evidence that was covered up. I finished with how the pictures could have been some kind of leverage.

The FBI agent then put an end to the discussions with the statement, "I don't want to go after old, dead cops."

That was it, and I sat there quietly hiding my state of total frustration and disillusionment. It was over—I couldn't hand it off to someone appropriate. I don't know the duties and expectations on a federal agent, but when you're a local law enforcement officer, there is nothing bigger and more important than a murder, and this one was of one of the most driving of victims. Lisa was a teenager, a wonderful young person yet to live out the rest of the moments of a full life. This would be the number one focus of a local police department, and little manpower or expense would be spared. I thought I was at the end—the last hope of obtaining justice for a sixteen-year-old girl seemed to be ready to walk out the door on me. I was hiding depression.

In the seconds lapsing while I descended into frustration and disillusionment, it suddenly became apparent I had forgotten one important thing: I had forgotten that I was not the only former small-town cop sitting at that table.

"Mike, keep working this case," my acquaintance said, breaking the uncomfortable silence that had descended on the meeting. He would not have entertained my ideas and set up the meeting if he did not see the same things I was seeing. It was, at that moment, the most frustrating thing I could have heard.

I didn't want this on my hands as a private citizen anymore with the potential implications. I had tried to hand this case off to multiple agencies, showing both of them that there was a "there" there. In that moment, I was very frustrated, but would gradually find the true silver lining in that cloud. He encouraged me to obtain the Cuyahoga County Prosecutor's files on the case, and he didn't think that would get me into any trouble.

I thanked the men and we wrapped up the meeting. In the end, maybe I did get what the case really needed—encouragement and direction.

I don't know whether it is more appropriate to call this the birth or the evolution of what I'll refer to as "Me PD." Please know the moniker was born much more out of cynicism than ego. Also, know that this would not be the last time the Federal Bureau of Investigation would fail this case.

CHAPTER 14 : THE MISSING PICTURES

The prosecution file from Kevin's trial didn't take too long to arrive via email. I was thankful we were now in the digital age and it did not require mailing me over five thousand pages of documents in addition to copies of any pictures. I pictured a clerk at an old copy machine and wondered how thick the stack would have been decades ago. It was likely now at a scanner once for the files nowadays. Seeing the first link leading to what looked like thousands of pages of scanned documents, I clicked on the second link, which wound up being the photo file.

I scrolled down through all the photos. There were pictures of evidence taken in packaging, clothes, rusty old knives, a pair of boat shoes. There was a section that seemed to be of clothing evidence, likely taken at the coroner's office. Then there were pictures taken of the outdoor crime scene. I scanned through all the pictures that would have been taken at the scene on the day of murder and something hit me like a wrecking ball.

I went back to the photo files Renner had shared with me the previous year. None of the pictures Renner shared with me were found in the prosecution's file—*exactly none*. No pictures from inside the Dreifort residence; nor were there Polaroids from the searches of Kevin's house and dorm. This suggested to me immediately that there was a division of the pictures between those given to the prosecution and those kept somewhere else. But why? Wouldn't copies have been made? You couldn't have made copies of Polaroid instants, but 35mm film came with negatives. Did this mean the pictures Renner forwarded me had been kept back at the police department to be digitized decades later? None of the pictures of significance I found in Renner's cache were there in the official prosecution record of Kevin's aggravated murder trial.

I moved to the documents, and soon found the intimidating thousands of pages of documents to be a little less fearsome. Many pages were total black rectangles of redaction. I would go on to find there were many pages that contained the same things in duplicate, triplicate, and even a few instances of quadruplicate. It also made a big difference to skip over anything that looked like court documents; I was looking for things that led up to the trial, not so much the trial itself.

After many clicks of the mouse, I came across some facsimile memos sent by Kevin's defense attorney Mark DeVan to Deputy Chief James Brosius on May 7 and 10 of 1993 as Kevin's trial date approached. The first was a request to send items of physical evidence to who seemed like an independent forensic examiner, Dr. Peter DeForest. The items listed include Lisa's clothing; any footwear casts or inked impressions; any shoes seized or photographs of shoes seized; Dan Dreifort's t-shirt; the paper bag with blood and footwear impression; and the condom and wrapper found. It seemed to make sense to me—except for the fact that Renner's picture cache showed a clear plastic bag on the ground with potential blood tracks on it. This memo was the first indication as to why, in Renner's book, this crucial evidence was listed as a paper bag. This discrepancy fell to the wayside as I read the very short memo dated May 10, 1993. The text of the message reads as follows:

This letter will supplement our letter of May 7, 1993. As I indicated during our telephone conversation of that day, certain photographs are missing from those which you previously provided. Please forward the following missing photographs: #1, #2, #7, #17, #24, #25, #26, #31.

This memo seemed like a bombshell, the first documented indication that something was wrong. A defense attorney with an aggravated murder trial approaching was indicating that he had not been given certain pictures. What I could not find was how the pictures would have been numbered for purposes, and how DeVan would have identified which pictures and corresponding numbers he did not have. Nothing in Renner's cache or the prosecution file came with any corresponding numbers. I did not find any grand list describing each photo. Could the numbers have come from the negatives? The pictures were numbered somehow, and there had to be quite a lot of them, but the ones DeVan claimed were missing were eight of the first thirty-one on whatever list there was.

The next thing of significance were two pages of what seemed like copies of fronts of old film processing envelopes, both with the logo of "One Hour Motophoto." The dates on both envelopes were 01-03-91, and consecutive serial numbers are observed on the envelopes. Both are marked "S.H.P.D." and request "2 sets of 5x7, glossy, each negative." The first envelope is marked for 72 prints of Kodak 35mm film with 200 speed. The second envelope is marked for 28 prints of "Koni" film with no size or speed checked. The "Koni" must correspond to Konica film, but the 28-print order puzzles. Film rolls were typically sold in 12, 24, and 36 exposure rolls. Seventy-two prints of Kodak film makes sense, a multiple of typical 35mm rolls—twenty-eight does not. Remembering the days of film developing, a roll of film often could have an extra exposure on them, making for more than the listed number of pictures returning on an order.

The first thing that became apparent was that the date on the photo-processing envelopes tells us something. The pictures of a September 14 murder were not developed until January 3 of the following year, a gap of more than three and a half months. What was in these pictures was obviously not taken into consideration in the early days of the investigation when the focus was narrowed down to one young man, Kevin Young.

I began to count up only those taken at the outdoor scene and inside the Dreifort house from the crime scene photos between Renner's cache and the prosecution file. Trying to eliminate duplicate images, I came up with total number of film prints for each section. From Renner's cache, I counted twenty-two images taken outdoors, twenty-nine taken inside the Dreifort residence, and fifteen of Kevin's dorm room; and then counted thirty-four prints from the prosecutor's office files of the outdoor crime scene. Those numbers added up to one hundred, which exactly matches the number of prints ordered between the two photo envelopes.

The difference between the two photo-processing envelopes now came into focus. The envelope for Kodak film has "speed" and "size of film" boxes checked by the clerk, and a prints number of 72. As established, 35mm film cannisters were typically sold in 12, 24, and 36 exposure rolls, so the 72 makes perfect sense as a multiple or combination of different exposure rolls. The envelope marked by the clerk does not indicate any size or speed of the film, and lists it as "Koni," which, again, is presumably Konica film. It lists the strange number of 28 prints, and the clerk and photo processing business would likely charge by exposure. Researching old Konica film rolls, I found the typical 12, 24, and 36 exposure rolls and even a rare instance of 15 exposure rolls. If I found any 14 or 28 exposure rolls of any size film, it would correspond to a full roll for this photo order. This led me to the conclusion that with this order, a full roll was not given to the clerk, but just sets of negatives. The clerk wouldn't know a size or speed, as they would be easily found on the roll. Therefore, I propose that if we add 8 to the total of 28, we get 36, which would represent a typical roll, or combination of rolls, of film. Eight was the number of photos listed as missing by defense attorney Mark DeVan in the memo.

I would love to see the backsides of these photos, to see which correspond to which brand of film, and account for things that way, and a full set of negatives may accomplish the same thing. Eight pictures would also make the difference between the film prints listed between all the files I had seen and the number 108, which would be a multiple of 12 and correspond to three rolls of 36 exposure film, or some combination, perfectly. It is harder to make this argument without confirmation that no images of our juvenile victim's exposed body were taken. The negatives and backs of the pictures indicating film manufacturer could tell us a lot more.

What we do know is there is a memo alleging missing pictures, and certain pictures not found in the prosecution's file could have had the power to prevent this trial. What I will now add is that the pair of Chuck Taylor All-Star shoes on that wooden floor were the only shoes I saw photographed in any of the files that were not held up for the camera to take close-up photos of them or to take pictures of their soles. Every other pair of shoes in question in these photos were held up and had their soles photographed. Reading DeVan's memo alleging missing pictures, I noticed the consecutive numbers 24, 25, and 26 listed as missing. My thoughts immediately went to those three pictures of Chuck Taylors on that wooden floor. They were three slightly different images by the details; they had to be three consecutive clicks of a camera's shutter. I found no other explanation of the numbering in the memo than that the numbers had to be numbers on negatives, and #24, #25, and #26 might correspond to pictures of the shoes.

Maybe most frustratingly, the one picture I immediately wanted after finding that rare, old version of a pair of shoes which got me started was not there. No picture of the footwear impression, supposedly made in blood, was found in the prosecution's file for the trial of Kevin Young. It had not been in Renner's cache either. Why would something that would constitute the most important piece of physical evidence linking a suspect and the crime not be found in any of the pictures? Numerous pieces of evidence were photographed individually. Why not this most important bag?

Twenty-eight plus eight will always equal thirty-six, and I can think of eight pictures I saw that would start to put the case against Kevin Young into question: pictures of the Chuck Taylor shoes, the back porch, and a plastic bag. These eight pictures show potential blood evidence not sent to the FBI Laboratory. The locations of these pieces of evidence are both immediately outside, and inside the Dreifort residence.

CHAPTER 15 : THE DEVIL'S HAIRCUT (MAPP VS OHIO VS SHAKER HEIGHTS)

In the late 1980s, a man by the name of Ed Leslie got himself on television by wrestling professionally under the name Brutus Beefcake. It was a good name, but he became even more famous when he came up with a good gimmick. He modified the name to Brutus "the Barber" Beefcake and began to routinely finish his matches by applying a sleeper hold to render his opponents "unconscious," at which point he would gleefully begin to cut their hair to the delight of the live audience. The reason I bring this up is not for levity; rather, it might actually figure into the "how" and "why" of this murder.

I pointed out to the Shaker Heights detective that Renner's book mentioned that on the day preceding the murder, Daniel Dreifort repeatedly expressed the fantasy of cutting Lisa's hair to his liking. Daniel even mentions this in his official police statement, though he downplays it. He listed the desire to cut her hair short like his, but that Lisa liked her hair long. The official statement of friend Kenny Workman reflects a confirmation of this fantasy, but Workman likewise tries to play it down, insisting Dreifort was "just playin' around."

The story included that Daniel wanted Kenny to physically hold Lisa down during this haircut. When asked if Daniel was holding scissors when making the statement, he said that Daniel was holding clippers. Kenny would later admit telling multiple people that he initially believed Daniel killed Lisa. It seemed obvious that no teenage girl would want her hair cut by her boyfriend, especially not at night and not something extreme. This reminded me of a recent scandal in the Amish community where certain Amish men were targeted for "beard cutting" against their will. I pointed out to the detective that this would be akin to an act of violence against a woman, and was also a possible reason a sharp object would have been near Lisa Pruett that night.

Reading the coroner's autopsy report for Lisa, I found two things interesting. Lisa was found to have bruising on one side of her neck. I wondered if that could be consistent with a sleeper hold, since Daniel would have been alone with Lisa, no Kenny to hold her down. I believe Kenny wanted no part of the haircut idea and made other plans. He had a very solid alibi of being at his residence on the phone with his girlfriend (Dan's sister Deborah Dreifort) at the time of the murder. Reading the text describing the stab wounds, I wondered if they could describe an object without sharp edges, such as a closed pair of scissors, making the wounds.

Mapp vs Ohio is one of the most important US Supreme Court decisions in history with regards to criminal law and law enforcement. It actually originated from a case in Cleveland, the immediate neighbor of Shaker Heights, and set standards for search and seizure in criminal cases, and the requirements of search warrants. Search warrants take some time to prepare and obtain in the daytime. Obtaining a search warrant at night during an investigation would involve diverting manpower to prepare it, then finding and waking up a judge. No search warrant was found for the

Dreifort residence in the prosecution file. The investigators were likely working on a consent search for the pictures taken inside the Dreifort house.

The first search warrant issued in this murder investigation was issued less than forty-eight hours after Lisa's body was found early Sunday morning, September 16, 1990. It was for the residence where Kevin Young lived. It was issued by Shaker Heights Municipal Court, which made sense in that it shared the same municipal building as the police. Kevin's defense attorneys would later challenge the probable cause for this warrant, maybe rightfully so, even though nothing implicating Kevin was ever determined to be found from it. Having obtained a few search warrants, I thought the probable cause was highly questionable, but assumed that any issuing authority might not want to look bad in the murder of a teenage girl.

It was not the probable cause listed to obtain the search warrant that I really cared about once I saw the list of items police sought authority to seize. The items to seize explicitly listed shoes with herringbone soles, and a knife or *scissors.* How did they know to specify scissors? Did the coroner's office or autopsy report specifically tip the investigators off to that? Was it another reason? It was my contention and conviction that police had the Frankenstein shoes with herringbone heels and a boyfriend with a fantasy of cutting her hair who was supposed to be outside with Lisa at 2940 Lee Road, not at the Youngs'.

Renner's photo cache included two that seemed to be of a back patio with metal chairs nestled in the corner of a brick building, which would later match the rear of 2940 Lee Road in Zillow real estate photos. There was a brick windowsill loaded with items, one appearing to be some kind of radio. I noticed a long orange line which corresponded to an outdoor extension cord. On top of a little bin was a small gray item with an apparent black power cord coming out one end that I was certain was a set of barber's clippers. The official statement of Kim Rathbone indicated she had cut Daniel's hair short on the sides, and her answer to a question indicated they had been outside, just the two of them. It had to be on that back porch with the extension cord, chairs, and clippers, right? Those clippers were photographed as being left out into the dark night hours, sometime between one a.m. and sunrise.

The most important thing I found in these two photos, despite the photographer concentrating on an old pair of shoes left out near the edge of the house, were one large and multiple small drops of a red substance near the back of one of the patio chairs. A chair where a person might have been seated to receive a haircut with the extension cord and clippers right there. We will never know what these red drops actually were because they were not paid attention to, not photographed closely, not marked with evidence markers, not collected, and not sent to the FBI Laboratory. They were "potential blood evidence" not logged at the scene of a violent stabbing of a teenage girl. That is a damning statement in and of itself, and tells us something.

Moving to the Cuyahoga County Coroner's Office autopsy report for Lisa Lee Pruett gave me a couple of nuggets to ponder. The report lists four stab wounds to the posterior thorax of the victim. In describing these four wounds, the last sentence of the section states, "The sides are non-abraded." I was left pondering what that described in reference to a possible weapon in relation to these wounds. What did that tell us about the weapon as far as its edges? Could it have alluded to closed scissors? The search warrant had to have a reason to list scissors.

The section on the neck of the victim may shed the most light. It starts with indicating a "patterned focally abraded contusion on the anterior and lateral neck." Lisa had been wearing a long-sleeved blue turtleneck, which could have covered the majority of her neck for a cool night bike ride. It was there in the coroner's photographs, with markers for each stab wound. The fabric of her turtleneck was likely responsible for the patterned abrasions as the neck of the shirt was compressed against her skin. It was only on the front and sides of her neck. One could guess that her turtleneck was pulled from behind, but consider possibly the most important sentence in this section. The injury on the right neck is continuous with a more linear contused abrasion over the anterior and left neck.

If Ed Leslie had come out in his wrestling tights with a pair of scissors tucked somewhere on or nearby him and placed a serious sleeper hold on someone, it could have left marks similar to this. He would have wrapped his left arm around the neck from behind and drawn his left hand up as far as he could behind the right side of a victim's head, then using his left hand to clench his right bicep or elbow area. His right hand would have forced the victim's head down into his left forearm, putting considerable pressure on the right side of the victim's neck into a harder, more linear area of his left forearm.

A second search warrant was executed on the Young residence on October 19. Curiously, the items listed in this second warrant were knives of a certain size, but left out any explicit mention of scissors, unlike the first search warrant. The search warrant executed on Kevin's dorm room in Columbus, likewise, only lists a knife of a certain size to be seized, the second exclusion of the mention of scissors. Brutus "the Barber" Beefcake was in the public lexicon of many adolescent boys in the late 1980s. Could Ed Leslie's gimmick alter ego have helped us explain the truth of Lisa's death?

Later, I found paperwork in the file releasing the personal property of Lisa from the Cuyahoga County Coroner's Office. Listed were a broken multi-colored beaded necklace, a white metal chain noted as being similar to one military dog tags would be on, and a broken black-and-white string band. This list gives us more to ponder with regards to the bruising around the victim's neck and jaw. The coroner's report lists the marks as "abraded contusions." Coroners and medical examiners are all experienced on identifying ligature marks when evidence points to something restraining or strangling a victim. The neck section does not make mention anything resembling a ligature, only abraded contusions. Examination of the actual autopsy photos of the neck may be more effective answering this question. Could a necklace or chain pulled from one direction create this bruising? If so, would it make evidence more consistent with a ligature rather than bruising? It would be useful for future investigations to examine any neck photos to see if the bruising is more consistent with a ligature from the necklace or chain, or if it were more explainable by some kind of choke or sleeper hold applied from behind the victim.

CHAPTER 16 : THE TELL-TALE SHIRT

I didn't spent much time on the photos of Lisa's clothing. Nothing stood out on first glance. There were pictures displayed of male clothing, presumably that of Kevin Young, acquired on search warrants. Then there were numerous pictures of Lisa's turtleneck, blue jeans, and panties with coroner's office labels and scale markers indicating perforations from stab wounds. Taking a second and third look at things had paid off in this case before for me, so it was worth taking another look at these definite pieces of physical evidence.

Lisa had been wearing a long-sleeved blue turtleneck for her nighttime bicycle ride to Dan's house. Now it was captured in numerous pictures on a wire hanger suspended on a metal pole in the coroner's office photos. A ruler-like scale with the case number and date accompanied each piece of clothing in each picture, with smaller, arrow-like markers with both letters and numbers indicating perforations suspected to be stab wounds. Putting these pictures and the Cuyahoga County Coroner's report together brings us to some reasonable findings and some new, more puzzling questions.

The neck of the shirt seems to not be stretched out in any way, almost like it was still in a drawer and had never been worn. If it had been grabbed to pull the victim for restraining or choking, it would likely seem stretched out or deformed in some direction, which it was not. This supports my theory of a chokehold or sleeper hold being applied to Lisa's neck, causing the strange bruising. If something like her collar, a necklace, or something wrapped around her neck to choke her, it is very likely the coroner's report would reflect ligature marks on the neck. This assertion was not present.

Lisa's fatal wounds were listed as penetrating wounds of her left lung and aorta, the main artery of the body. Four stab wounds are listed on the left posterior thorax between 48 and 53 inches above the heel. They are described as vertically inclined, and in each instance, the instrument passed somewhat upward from back to front to a depth of two-and-a-half to two-and-three-quarters-inches deep. The reports numbers them one through four starting from upper to lower, and notes the dimensions as 5/8", 7/16", 5/8", and 5/8" respectively. The three larger defects are said to display a sharp angle superiorly and a straight angle inferiorly, and that the sides are non-abraded. The three larger defects are reported to penetrate the victim's thoracic wall, either between or through rib bones, and pierce the upper and lower lobe of the left lung.

Looking at the photos of Lisa's shirt, we first must understand that fabric, and even skin and flesh, can be flexible and stretch a bit. A piece of clothing can stretch, fold, or be moved over different spots on a body. Looking at the rear of the shirt, we see five perforations, all mostly vertically made, on the left portion of the rear of the shirt, and they are marked with arrow markers R, S, T, U and V. The first curiosity becomes the difference between the five marked perforations on the shirt in an area where the coroner lists four stab wounds. The second curiosity seems that the tears to the shirt all seem a bit lower than they should be to correspond to the wounds on the body, and this may indicate shirt was pulled up a bit in a struggle.

The relative positioning of these wounds on the shirt may be revealing. T, U, and V seem to be in a small random cluster corresponding to wounds 3 and 4 on the coroner's report, which puncture the lower lung. Why three wounds on the shirt and two on the body is a good question I cannot answer. Folding over a section of the shirt could lead to one stab producing two or three tears in the fabric, and evidence will show that her shirt was pulled up.

Tears R and S may reveal something very important in that they do not show the randomness the other three do. They correspond to the wound to the victim's upper lung lobe. R and S appear to clearly be different lengths, but the most telling fact is they appear to not be random in respect to each other. They appear to perfectly line up with each other, end to end, so perfectly that it is highly unlikely to be random. It is my contention that these two tears to Lisa's shirt were made by one instrument, a pair of opened scissors. Remember that a pair of scissors was explicitly listed as a potential weapon to seize in the first search warrant in this case, issued less than forty-eight hours after the crime.

Turning to a different piece of clothing affirms the assertion that the shirt was being pulled up in the commission of the stabbing. Two perforations of the lace of each cup of the victim's bra are marked by the arrow pointer labels of the coroner's office in photos. Turning back to the front of the blue turtleneck, there are no corresponding perforations of the front of the shirt in the breast area. The victim was said to have been found with the turtleneck pushed up over her bra, and it must have been pushed up that way for the stab wounds to her breast area, one of which punctured her aorta.

Let me step back to our school days of simple math, fractions, and ratios. Examining the photos of Lisa's shirt and using the scale in the photographs, I get measurements of approximately 0.66" (slightly more than 5/8") and 0.96" for shirt wounds R and S respectively, which I remind you line up perfectly enough that they cannot be random. If you want to look at the difference in the sizes as a ratio, it would come out as 1 to 1.45. Going back to the coroner's measures, there were three wounds of 5/8" and 7/16". The ratio of those two numbers is 1.43 to 1. I believe this fact is a deceiving coincidence. The puzzling thing is the coroner lists the second of the four wounds moving downward as the small 7/16" wound, where the shirt suggests R would be the smaller wound and be on top. We have to keep in mind that many things depend on the angles of any wounds, and if the shirt were stretched, folded, moved, or compressed. Many things could affect the size of the wounds, but the alignment of wounds R and S to the shirt cannot be ignored.

Photos of the victim's panties show two different stories in apparent blood, though there is hardly any on this item for belonging to a stabbing victim. There appears to be two small areas of blood on the front of the panties which appear, to me, to be two blood drops dripped from somewhere directly above the panties at the time. I cannot tell from photos if these drops would have landed on the outer or inner surface of the front area of the panties.

The band of the right leg opening of the panties which would normally sit at the juncture of the right inner thigh and the crotch/vaginal area shows a darker red staining of the opening's band for a length and that darker red staining is seen on a smaller portion of the fabric along this length of the band. The victim was found with her jeans and panties pulled completely off the left leg and bunched around the right ankle area of her right leg, but the coroner's office did not find evidence of sexual assault or any stab wounds to the leg or lap areas. These facts led me to believe that the panties may have been pulled over an area of blood and that the inner leg band collected some of this blood during the act that must have happened after the stabbing.

What could explain the differences in the punctures on the back of the victim's shirt to the stab wounds listed in the coroner's report?

I started looking around my residence and found I owned two pairs of scissors, a common utility pair and a slimmer pair of barber's scissors that came with a clipper set. When I opened these scissors to where the blades made a ninety-degree angle, both sets of blades measured between two and a half and two and three-quarters inches, the same as noted for depths of the four stab wounds on Lisa's back that punctured her lungs. When I measured the widths of the blades near their hinge junctures, the utility scissors measured roughly 5/8 of an inch, the barber scissors measured roughly 7/16 of an inch, the exact lengths of the four stab wounds to her back listed by the coroner.

Many common household scissors have a wider, stouter top blade and a smaller, thinner lower blade. The top blade commonly has a blunted end that slopes from the blunt outer edge down to the tip of the sharp bladed edge. The smaller, lower blade typically is thinner and makes a straighter line on the outer dull edge to the point where it meets the bladed edge at the tip. Reading the coroner's report again, the three larger stab wounds to her left back, measured at 5/8", had a sharp angle superiorly, straight angle inferiorly. This now seems very consistent with the blunted end of the upper blade of a pair of scissors, either alone or with the blades closed.

To explain the difference in the length of longer shirt puncture S and the corresponding smaller stab wound 2, take out a pair of scissors and either a piece of paper or a piece of fruit you're about to eat. Take your scissors and open the blades about an inch or so, and slowly stab into the paper or fruit with the blades open. As both blades plunge into the surface, the distance between the blades at the surface gradually decreases, eventually to zero at the juncture of the blades. One of the surface stab holes will have to increase in size and approach the other stab hole end to end in order to accommodate the closing of distance between the two blades. This explains why shirt tear S is so much longer than it needs to be. The smaller bottom blade of a pair of scissors would have made the 7/16" wound listed as the second descending wound to her back, but the closing of the blades would have torn a bigger defect into the shirt at the surface even with this smaller blade. The ratios I wasted our time with were coincidental as proved by simple logic. The top blade being 5/8" in width easily fits into both top shirt tear R and 5/8" stab wound 1 on the victim's back. A smaller lower blade of the scissors could easily have made stab wound 2, then cut a larger slash towards the upper blade's perforation as the two blades came closer together as they were pushed deeper. As I plunged my utility scissors, blades opened between one and one and a half inches, the marks in my sacrificial grapefruit closely match perforations R and S on the back of Lisa Pruett's blue turtleneck, the lower blade having to tear that longer perforation at the surface directly at the top perforation. In addition, the coroner's report indicates that the 7/16" second stab wound from the top did not puncture the thoracic wall, so it may not have gone in as deep, or gone in at a shallower angle. From the far opposite ends of R and S measures 1.86", and the small, uncut gap between the inner ends of the two perforations measures 0.23", which is easily achievable by a pair of scissors or shears, opened a little less than 1.5" being plunged into something to a depth of two and a half inches.

These four stab wounds to Lisa Pruett's left back can now be viewed as absolutely consistent with being made by a pair of common scissors or shears. Who had a reason to have scissors near her that night? There was a young man who was never more than one hundred feet away from this crime with a fantasy of cutting this young woman's hair, but he was strangely and overly protected by the city of Shaker Heights to the media.

CHAPTER 17 : THE SHELL GAME

DNA as a forensic tool first became a reality in the United Kingdom in 1986, so it would not be an understatement to say that the technology was barely more than a toddler in the years of 1990 and 1991. Many police departments did not have local access to good forensic examination and technicians, and many departments sent important evidence to the FBI Laboratory for examination. This case was no different, and forensic examinations can often take months to complete, depending on the workload and backlog of the examining agency. I can certainly imagine the FBI Laboratory of the early 1990s to have no shortage of work from important cases from across an entire nation.

The prosecution file contained a facsimile memo from the FBI Laboratory dated March 5, 1991. The first two items listed were from the scene, identified as items Q1 and Q2. Q1 is described as a *"Plain Dealer* Magazine" and a number "1" is followed in parentheses. The *Plain Dealer* has been the leading Cleveland area newspaper for generations, and on Fridays and Sundays, there was an extra "magazine" insert which was usually smaller. Q2 is described as a "brown paper bag" with a number "2" after it in parentheses. Other items listed included a blood and hair sample from Kevin Young, tissue paper, a blood sample from our victim, and her clothing worn that day. The first page listed that human bloodstains, sufficient in amount for DNA profiling, were identified on Q2, and would later be addressed in the shoe print section of the report.

There it was—confirmation that the most important piece of physical evidence was made upon a brown paper bag. Renner's book had mentioned this, with a *Plain Dealer* magazine being found inside the paper bag. This brown paper bag was nowhere to be found in either set of crime scene pictures I viewed. Neither the prosecution nor Renner's photos had contained an image of a brown paper bag with any impression as an individual piece of evidence, or on the ground at the crime scene. Renner's cache of photos contained two images which showed a clear plastic bag with a paper item inside, and two small rusty-brown areas on top of it which could correspond to a blood track. It was the focus of one of the photos; the second photo showed it amongst vegetation within feet of a house. I thought those two areas were small enough to be partials made from a portion of the heel of a shoe.

My first theory was that Renner had mixed up the semantics, as I believed the clear plastic bag was consistent with that commonly used by newspaper deliverers to protect periodicals typically thrown into a driveway or front yard against any elements. I thought "paper bag" could have had an alternate meaning of "bag for newspapers." But this lab report clearly stated that the piece of evidence was a brown *paper* bag, and the "brown" designation clearly eliminated the possibility the bag was made of anything other than paper. The pictures and documents started to show discrepancies.

Nothing of forensic value was obtained from any of the evidence submitted to the FBI lab, though other things about the report may be telling. The Q2 bloodstain was determined to be unable to provide results due to "insufficient and/or degraded DNA." There could be a number of reasons for this: packaging or storing error, the relative youth of DNA technology, or the properties of paper that could have possibly absorbed the blood. This could present an obstacle to the value of this evidence now in that it could be argued it cannot be positively matched to the victim's blood. The shoe print section of the report lists photographs were taken to be retained for future examinations by the FBI, and copies of the photos returned with the report. The next stanza indicates that the manufacturer or brand name of the shoe which made the impression of Q2 cannot be determined. The FBI is known to have had reference data with regards to footwear patterns, but it could be very possible that they would not have in their reference any example of a very rare version of a shoe such as the Frankenstein shoes.

I must interject now that I have never been able to obtain the two things I initially asked James Renner for when contacting him about the case. I have never found an evidence list from the search of the Dreifort residence or a copy of any photo of the blood impression on the paper bag. I don't understand how the most important pieces of evidence cannot be found in photo files. My subsequent Freedom of Information Act request for the FBI's copy of the photo of the blood impression was returned, acknowledging there was a record for it but that it could not be found. How can this happen? This should be the item that links this murder to the perpetrator. Its value can be questioned by the inability to get DNA results, which might be reversed by new generations of the technology. But we cannot compare it to anything if we have no pictures of it. So as of now, what should be something very important in this murder is just a ghost; there are multiple records of it, but we cannot see it. We also cannot see it at the crime scene.

The next document from the FBI Laboratory is dated July 19, 1991, and seemingly details a May 17, 1991, communication regarding shoe print analysis. Nothing of forensic value was determined from the analysis, but the contents again may tell us something. Nine plaster casts of footwear impressions were listed as being sent for analysis. Three pairs of actual footwear were apparently sent to the lab listed as belonging to William Misencik, George Campany, and Michael Kolat. I recognized Misencik's name from the book and police reports as an officer, and am assuming the other two names are officers related to the case. The last two items were listed as "inked impression of left (and subsequently right) Lotto sneaker belonging to DAN DREIFORT." What struck me as shockingly preposterous was that someone would send in their officers' actual footwear to a laboratory, but only inked impressions of a suspect's footwear. A homicide case should have involved the actual shoes, and there were no problems sending in officers' shoes. The report states none of the impressions matched any of the actual shoes submitted, but the inked impressions of the Lotto shoes were eliminated from all but Q12b. The report states that the inked impressions and Q12b could not be determined to be linked due to the "limited nature of the questioned impression and due to the indistinct nature of" the inked impressions. Curiously, the report states that a determination was not made whether the Q2 blood impressions were, or were not, made by any of the shoes or shoe impressions in question.

Going back to the cache of pictures Renner sent me, along with the prosecution's photo file, I can find no pictures of any kind of shoes matching a Lotto brand shoe. Lotto is an Italian brand of athletic shoes, and I looked up any old examples for sale. The section of photos taken inside the Dreifort residence contain a number of pictures taken inside what looks like the room of a teenage boy. I can see a collection of shoeboxes near a window, and a couple others in other pictures, but none of them are consistent with a Lotto brand shoebox of the period. The Lotto sneakers started to seem like another ghost. The typed-out and signed statement of Daniel Dreifort lists that he had been wearing his Chuck Taylor All-Stars the night of the murder up until 12:30 a.m., the accepted time of the murder. These are the shoes which needed to be eliminated by technicians at a laboratory. Why weren't they?

CHAPTER 18 : THE INADMISSIBLE

Lie detection technology and their tests represent the ultimate dichotomy in law enforcement. On one hand, they are very useful in identifying suspects, clearing people of suspicion, and eliciting admissions and confessions. There is definitely some science to it—using monitors for respiration, heart rate, skin conductivity, and sometimes voice stress. The opposite blade of that sword is their inadmissibility in nearly all cases in criminal court proceedings. Polygraphers strongly believe in their trade and abilities, but the overall reliability is not high enough to be used against a person being charged. There is some subjectivity in the evaluation of the tests.

In the prosecution's file, I found a four-page evaluation of the polygraph examinations conducted in this investigation. The evaluation was prepared by William D. Evans II of Poly-Tech Associates Incorporated. Evans' evaluation does not list any specific questions asked of any of the examinees, but there are some things we can learn from these pages. The listed names of examinees include David Branigan, Stanley Kramer, Holly Robinson, Dan Messinger, Rebecca Boatright, Robert Dreifort, Kent Mitsumoto, Chris Jones, Daniel Dreifort, Kevin Young, and Kenny Workman. Branigan, Kramer, Robinson, Messinger, Boatright, and Jones seem to be on the list as people who either overheard information about the get-together Daniel Dreifort was planning that night at his house or were explicit invitees. Robert Dreifort, Daniel Dreifort, Kevin Young, and Kenny Workman seem like they were on the informal suspect list for reasons of proximity, knowledge, or other statements.

The summation of Evans' report reveals his opinions that the methodology of the examinations renders their results inconclusive. Without repeating every word of his report, I will try to echo his conclusions with what I read. Evans lists the tests of Branigan, Kramer, Robinson, Messinger, and Boatright as "no deception indicated," with one test being administered each, except in the case of Branigan, who had two. He lists Mitsumoto and Jones' single tests as inconclusive for different reasons. He finds slight deception or deception on two questions asked to Robert Dreifort and Kevin Young, while finding the same on three questions asked to Kenny Workman. He lists problems with not having control questions to gauge against relevant questions in these tests. He has two tests administered on Daniel Dreifort. With the first, he opines that there are greater reactions on control questions than on the relevant questions, which seems strange. He believes the second test reveals deceptive answers on relevant questions but cannot find control questions to judge them against.

These statements all go to support his general assertion of inconclusiveness in what he sees in the examinations. Four subjects appeared to have some deceptive answers, but they certainly could not have all perpetrated the crime, which suggests these results are meaningless. Kenny Workman has the best alibi of anyone with a documentable phone call between his residence and girlfriend Deborah Dreifort's Ohio University dorm room, which overlapped the time of commission of this murder. His deceptive answers show the imperfections of the technology, as do those of Young and the Dreiforts. We don't have any record to see the questions asked or any of the data.

Rather than delving into confusing issues of methodology on something that is both inadmissible and inexact, I offer Evans' independent report to shine light on the issue of simple logic that multiple people had deceptive answers on the polygraphs, and that they could not all have perpetrated the crime or conspired together to do so. It appears that no person should have been excluded as a suspect based on the results, according to Evans.

Kevin Young's parents offered to take lie detector tests for the investigation to support Kevin's alibi. Kevin's father was a practicing attorney who allowed his son to be interviewed, polygraphed, and have physical evidence taken from him without argument. The difference between a polygraph being administered to Robert Dreifort versus none to the Youngs may be that the Youngs were not considered potential suspects, whereas Robert Dreifort was at one time considered a person lower on the list of suspicion because of proximity to the crime. It doesn't appear the polygraphs were entertained to support an alibi of another, otherwise the Youngs and Jean Dreifort could have been tested.

CHAPTER 19 : THE MYSTERY OF MARK DEVAN

"Well, they never took the shoes!"

It was late spring, mid-May 2024, when I made the decision to look up Kevin's defense attorneys, Mark DeVan and J. Michael Murray. From the website for the firm of Berkman, Gordon, Murray and DeVan, I found an email listed for DeVan. I wrote to him that I had begun an independent investigation into the case and believed I had uncovered enough evidence to determine what did and did not happen. I was inquiring if he still had an archive from the case in his possession with photos obtained in discovery. I asked to be allowed to independently examine any collection of crime scene photos that were given to him, without revealing why, to independently verify if he were ever given the photos I had seen, which should have prevented Kevin's trial. It was my working theory, at the time, that these photos were likely not given to the defense attorneys. I thought he would be very interested to hear what I had to say.

I never heard back.

After my summer presentation to the Cuyahoga County prosecutors, I was left with the nagging impression nothing could be done without the assistance of Shaker Heights Police. I mulled around possible ideas to help the case or put spotlight on it, and needed any advice I could muster. There was media coverage, of course. My mind went back to the original attorneys. Wouldn't they have be interested in what I found? Wouldn't they want to help in any way they could? DeVan and Murray were heroic figures in this case, at least to a few, including James Renner and myself. They were the Atticus Finches of this story, defending a factually innocent young man on the largest of state stages against the heaviest of charges under the laws of society. I reasoned that they would be amongst the best advice I could get in the private sector.

I wrote two copies of the same letter, addressed one each to Murray and DeVan at the law firm's downtown address. I included copies of the four-page report I had submitted to the prosecutor's office and sent them off in the mail. Murray and DeVan lived this saga firsthand for years, spending so much professional time on something this big had to cross over into the personal range, hadn't it? I began to wait; again, not certain this step would produce any reaction or advice that could help find the truth. It was perfectly conceivable they no longer kept an archive or any pictures on the case.

Weeks later, I began a fall hike at my favorite park to enjoy the October foliage and forest when my phone began to ring. I pulled it out of my pocket to reveal a call from a 216 area code, which usually covers the city of Cleveland and its county, Cuyahoga. My hope was that a certain local journalist I had been referred to was finally contacting me.

I opened the phone and said, "Hello?"

"Hi, Mike… this is Mark DeVan."

I thanked him for the response and we began a brief conversation. He had read my letter and final report, and expressed an interest in seeing these pictures I had mentioned. I began to speak about what I had found as far as footwear evidence when DeVan very abruptly and naturally blurted out something I had been looking for for more than nine months at that time.

"Well, they never took the shoes!"

I will never forget that statement because it was a near-*Eureka!* moment for me in establishing some sort of confirmation or corroboration of what I knew *had* to be true. In my first reading of *Little, Crazy Children*, the biggest question on my mind was if they had actually taken Dan Dreifort's shoes for examination and elimination in relation to the blood imprint found on a paper bag. I even posed this question to Renner in one of my first couple emails to him, so suspicious of Dreifort and laser-focused on that blood imprint as the key. When the Google searches I had done popped up with the images of this one pair of Frankenstein shoes, it elevated my suspicion into a conviction, a responsibility to follow this lead. Once again, I had to entertain and theorize the idea that his shoes were never examined as evidence.

The belief had solidified into rock when I found the crime scene photos in Renner's cache of the Chuck Taylor high tops with apparent blood and cough syrup on them. There was never any confirmation to be found in the prosecution files. No evidence lists, no supplemental reports from detectives detailing what they found, examined, or seized were ever uncovered in the prosecutor's files I obtained. Most importantly, the photos of Dan Dreifort's shoes were not in the photo section of what Cuyahoga County's Prosecutor's Office returned to me in the FOIA request. Even with all these findings pointing me to that one undeniable conclusion, I still wanted to find some kind of official confirmation, either in the records or from someone involved in the case. DeVan had just done that. I felt an additional level of confidence come over my investigation, at least for that moment. DeVan cordially invited me to his office to review my findings, and we set a time for an afternoon the following week.

I prepared for my second presentation of Lisa's case that year and headed to downtown Cleveland with my file and one Frankenstein shoe in my satchel. I parked and walked to and then through Cleveland's Public Square, past monuments and trees, to 55 Public Square on its northwest corner. I entered the building and took the elevator up to the floor listed for Berkman, Gordon, Murray, and DeVan. In my mind, I was anticipating DeVan to be outraged at what I was about to show him. I was expecting him to be on my side. What ensued proved those expectations to be naïve and wrong, and began another mystery to which this day I cannot figure out.

I entered the law offices to a tremendous, high-floor view of downtown Cleveland and the Cuyahoga River Valley in a southward direction. The receptionist remarked about the view and offered me a water. Minutes later, DeVan walked out of the hallway and introduced himself. He directed me to a conference room and asked if I wanted a coffee, which I accepted. As we sat down at the conference room table, I started with an affable remark that I believed he was the first person I had ever met after reading about them in a book. I knew that I was sitting down with one of the premier defense attorneys of the region, a very intelligent and experienced person. I expected him to think as a defense attorney, hard-wired for decades.

We began to talk about the case, and I pulled the book, the Frankenstein shoe, and the relevant pictures from Renner's cache to gradually introduce to him. He had brought the copy of my report that I had mailed to him, and I noticed many areas highlighted in yellow. I showed him the shoe and told him how it had started me on my investigation. "I'm probably the only person in America that would spend ninety-eight dollars on this old pair of shoes," I said and laughed.

DeVan examined the shoes for a bit and asked me if they were Daniel Dreifort's shoes, to which, of course, I replied in the negative, but said they were evidence that Dreifort's shoes—which he admitted in his signed statement to wearing preceding the time of the murder—were made with an inexplicable herringbone heel. It was the beginning of the hardcore "defense attorneying" that I had not been expecting. I kept a cool that the twentysomething-year-old police officer I used to be may not have had. I was here for advice and hopefully help, not for debate or argument with a top-notch attorney. DeVan remarked that the heels on the shoes looked like it could have been an after-market modification. He was smart and prepared.

I replied that I did not believe that it was an individual modification due to how well the extra heel followed the profile of the rest of the heel so smoothly and perfectly. I believed an after-market modified shoe would show more evidence of being cut or shaved to shape, which the Frankenstein shoe's heel did not. It was too big of a coincidence to me, especially when I could match it to a partial impression from one of the castings taken at the scene.

We moved on to the pictures, which I had been assuming had not been shown to DeVan in a clearly illegal withholding of exculpatory evidence from the defense. I showed him progressively magnified images of the Chuck Taylor shoes, the back patio matching the Dreifort residence, and photos of a clear plastic bag with possible blood tracks on the ground.

DeVan left to return from his office with a magnifying glass to examine the pictures with. The one area of agreement we reached—surprising to me at the time—was that the pictures of the Dreifort back patio showed an extension cord and set of electric barber's clippers left outside into the dark early-morning hours after Daniel's own haircut, which was performed by neighbor Kim Rathbone on that very patio the previous evening. I explained that the picture supported my theory that Daniel ambushed Lisa with his violent haircutting fantasy on that very back porch and it led to the murder. Daniel would have needed scissors in addition to clippers for anyone with long hair, and the search warrant on the Young household the next day very specifically, and suspiciously, listed scissors to be seized if found. DeVan countered that it was just a sloppy house and the family left out something that should have been taken inside. It was possible, so then I moved to the sizeable drop, along with some smaller drops, of a red substance around a patio chair on the stone patio.

Then began a session of the repeated verse, "You don't know that." The extent of which I would later remark to another figure that if I heard the phrase again, my head might explode. DeVan was, of course, correct to assert this and that I did not know that the drops were blood. But I was correct in my follow-up questions to every "You don't know that." The follow-up questions, many of which I eventually just left in my mental holster to avoid a larger debate, would just elicit further "defense attorneying," which seemed increasingly more desperate and delusional. The red drops on the patio should have been photographed more closely, collected as possible evidence, and sent to the FBI Lab along with the other forensic evidence to determine what they were. I told DeVan that the pictures were evidence that a "fix was in," to which he gave his most disgusted facial expression in negative response. Those red drops were where they very well could be drops of blood from a person attacked while sitting in that chair, possibly after reacting with a scream when she realized someone was trying to give her a haircut in the dark. DeVan was in full-scale defense attorney mode, opining that the red drops on the ground could have been rust from the metal chair or some of the berries from the foliage, so I knew things would be pointless.

I moved to the pictures of a clear plastic bag on the ground with apparent blood tracks on its top side, near (but suspiciously not in the same position in both pictures) a white area on the ground I would later conclude had to be a plaster footwear casting. I pulled out the communication and reports from the FBI Laboratory to illustrate to DeVan that this item was not sent to the FBI, and the report listed the tell-tale footwear impression in blood as being on a *paper* bag, as I had read in Renner's book and thought for a while must have been his mistake. I pointed out that none of the pictures showed this paper bag. It was not in Renner's cache or the prosecution's files, and my later FOIA request to the FBI Laboratory was returned indicating they could not find the photo which was said to be kept on file in their documents.

DeVan countered that the bag was near Lisa's body, no photos of which would be disseminated due to her being a juvenile victim left exposed. He furthered that the clear plastic bag could have been some kind of packaging from investigative equipment left on the ground. But why would that have been photographed? Why would it show potential blood? I knew in my mind that there should have been many pictures of this blood impression, both at the scene and later as an individual piece of evidence. Where is this evidence? Why can't I get a picture of it, which should surely match the Frankenstein shoe? I didn't pose those questions to DeVan, and moved on to what I considered the holy grail, the photo which should have prevented Kevin's trial and led to the conviction of Daniel Dreifort.

I presented the magnified photo of the Chuck Taylor All-Stars matching what Daniel stated he had worn the night before. I made sure to quicky produce the Zillow real estate image taken from inside the residence listed as 2940 Lee Road. I showed him how the image exactly matched the

Dreifort's foyer inside their front door down to the banister and a tell-tale dark floorboard near where the shoes sat. DeVan predictably told me that I didn't know that was blood, after I specifically mentioned cardiopulmonary blood from a chest cavity. He went on a long personal story about staining the floor on a boat, after which an acquaintance had joked to him about how it looked like he had blood on his shoe. My discipline had worn thin, and I asked him if his girlfriend was stabbed to death seventy-five feet away during this story. He laughed and quipped, "I should hope not."

DeVan then moved the conversation to the absolute crescendo, the apex of what I thought to be desperation. "Mike, how do we know those are Dan Dreifort's shoes?"

When I thought I couldn't have been taken aback any more, that was laid on me. I replied that they matched what Dreifort stated he was wearing in his official signed statement and that I had matched the floor to the front foyer of his residence at the time; what more would I have needed? DeVan opined that they could belong to the father or his sister. I simply replied that the sister was away at college at the time. The session was grinding to the end.

Holding the photo, I asked, "What do you do when you find a piece of evidence like this?"

DeVan responded that after photographing, you would put it in proper packaging.

"No," I shot back.

A little experience gives a different answer. "You're calling your officer in charge because you're itching to make an arrest."

"So, you don't think this is the answer to this crime?" I summarily asked.

"No, not at all," DeVan dismissed.

I sat, trying to take all of it in, and said, "Okay."

I moved to the topic of Robert Dreifort's unemployment at the time of the 1993 trial. I posed to DeVan that Robert Driefort was unemployed for seventeen months at the time he was on the witness stand in Kevin's trial. With two children in college, it makes no sense that this had been a willing separation or sabbatical from the Cleveland Clinic, and that the reason likely had to do with this case. He could have either interfered with his son's psychiatric records or personnel, or possibly been involved in theft or embezzlement to fund extortion, which the evidence seemed to allude to. DeVan would have none of that. Why were inked impressions of shoes not seen in photos or reports sent to the FBI Laboratory instead of the shoes listed in Daniel's statement and in the holy grail photos? DeVan shrugged it off.

At some point near the end, DeVan wanted to know which agencies I had taken the pictures and my reports to. I knew he was on a fact-finding mission of his own from early on. I gladly told him for the selfish reason that I believed the knowledge that I had spread the pictures and report around would protect me. Any reprisals of any kind would point to one place and draw attention to certain people. What these people would want to avoid most is that attention. A trusted person opined to me that they would try to discredit me, and it now seemed prophetic. I had no clue it would start to come from the defense attorney of an innocent defendant. Another mystery was unfolding that I began to try to figure out within an hour.

"I may have seen these pictures," DeVan clearly stated.

With that, one of the region's premier defense attorneys put himself on top of an imaginary fence, one that cannot exist, between two bad options for him. It was my assumption that he hadn't, and that he would be outraged, but none of that would be found. If DeVan had stated he was never given these pictures, it would confirm all my suspicions and assertions in the case so far. If DeVan had stated he was given these pictures, he would have to admit he had information in discovery which should have prevented Kevin's trial, to which he could either be accused of failure or conspiracy. I had put a top-notch defense attorney into a no-win situation, and he could only put himself on that imaginary fence: he had to pick between admitting failure and admitting I was right.

He chose to do neither.

One more thing happened in that meeting that needs to be told. I brought up his confirmation that Dreifort's shoes had never been taken as evidence. He immediately issued a denial that he had told me that on the phone. As I have written in this chapter, that phone conversation is seared into my mind because it was something I had searched for confirmation on for my whole investigation and hadn't found. The shoes could not have been taken; I knew that the second the Frankenstein shoes popped up on that computer screen, and every step of progress supported and confirmed that. Now, this top-notch attorney had not only put himself on an imaginary fence between two bad choices, he had contradicted himself. It was no use saying or even thinking about debating; we just wrapped up our politely hostile meeting. There was one question I kept in the holster that would have been very probing to ask DeVan. *Have you been retained by any other figure in this case?*

DeVan should have been on my side, and the big question now was why he wasn't. My goal was to obtain advice and help, and it was clear he would give none of that—quite the opposite, with hostility. As total speculation, it might be a very smart move for any of the guilty parties to retain DeVan in this case.

I asked him his theory about the whole case since he had spent so much time and effort on it. I wanted to know what he thought happened to Lisa Pruett. Police and defense attorneys are meant to be antagonistic, the system is set up that way, but it often benefits one to think along the lines of the other. DeVan avoided any sense of playing detective, and veered toward what I would call a "canned" or "prefabricated" lawyer response that began with, "Well, they put this guy Tom Gray in charge of the case and…"

I don't really know what DeVan thought of me, but my mind turned off with that statement. The late Tom Gray was never, at any point, in charge. People can say that it's "your" case but that doesn't mean you absolutely have free rein when you're in police work—you have as much as is allowed you. I had the memo from DeVan to the person who was in charge, requesting "missing" pictures shortly before Kevin's trial. The truth was there, somewhere.

DeVan and I seemed to try our best to remain cordial to the end. I asked if he had any advice or help to give, and he had none. DeVan was not interested in keeping any of the information I had shown him. He told me none of the people I had contacted would call me back with the information I had. I told him I didn't want anyone to call me back. Inside, I knew I would refuse any communication with Shaker Heights. I am an outsider and any agency would not need help from me to make a case, though I would happily help if needed. As we got up to leave, I told DeVan it was nice to have met him, and there was both sincerity and sarcasm in the words. His parting words as he walked away were, "They never should have let you in the door."

I took none of it personally; I was too calmly perplexed trying to figure out what had just happened. It was a lot of hostility to give a volunteer of a noble cause. I held back many retorts. *I shouldn't have been let in the door?* What agency would ever refuse to hear possible information on a major crime? That would be failure and negligence. Did he not realize the case had been reopened because of me? It may be the biggest irony of my journey for Lisa and Kevin how I was treated by DeVan versus how I was treated by law enforcement. No law enforcement official ever debated what I showed them led to a conclusion, yet the innocent defendant's attorney wanted to tear me to shreds. I couldn't have made up stranger fiction. I walked out of the Shaker Heights Police Department with the respect, maybe admiration of the senior detective. I now walked out of DeVan's office with vitriol. I'm glad I never wanted to go to law school.

In the end, I will give some charity and benefit of the doubt to Mr. Mark DeVan. He successfully defended an innocent young man from the most serious of charges. It may have been possible from lesser attorneys due to factual innocence and lack of evidence, but the Youngs went with a good choice, a smart choice. Maybe he feels his image could suffer somehow from my investigation, but my gut feeling is that he was not involved in any kind of conspiracy around this trial. The reason for this is the immediate and natural statement blurted out in the first minute of our first conversation on that phone call, that "they never took the shoes!" The statement he now denies making. Mark DeVan did not have the wondrous abilities of Google, and nobody had the imagination for the Frankenstein shoes. The excuses I had once reserved for fellow police I will now kindly and appropriately offer for Mark DeVan. It had been a *Rocky* moment—I was given time against one of the best, was battered (unexpectedly), and came out standing. I knew the people would have been on my side, and that's what would win at a trial.

CHAPTER 20 : OF CIVIL ACTION AND CIVILITY

Many laws are governed by what are known as statutes of limitations, which set legal timeframes for which criminal charges or civil actions must be filed. They can range from days or months for small infractions up to unlimited time for the ultimate criminal charges of homicide, in most cases. Their purpose is to set reasonable limits on how long into the future any charges or suits can be presented, as it becomes more difficult the more time has passed to give fair trial. Smaller issues and crimes go by the wayside after a reasonable amount of time.

I hadn't given much thought to the possibility of civil lawsuits regarding Lisa's death and what had transpired. The statute of limitations in Ohio for a wrongful death lawsuit to be brought by the appropriate parties is two years from the incident, which had long passed. It brought to mind memories of the civil case against O.J. Simpson after his criminal acquittal in the 1990s, a civil jury finding Simpson responsible for the deaths of his ex-wife Nicole Brown Simpson and Ronald Goldman after being acquitted by a criminal jury in one of the most sensational crimes of my lifetime. That civil action had to be brought within the statute of limitations for a wrongful death suit under California law, whereas the criminal charges for murder could have been filed at any point in perpetuity.

Kevin Young was not around anymore to explore what civil suits may have been able to be attempted in regards to him. I would have loved for him to still be alive—first of all, for his own sake and that of his family. Secondly, I lamented his death for the possibility that legal action filed under his name could expose the things I had found and lead to a truth being forced into a courtroom and maybe the public. Referencing a more local crime once dubbed a crime of the century, it was ultimately ruled that a relative of a prosecuted and imprisoned person could not sue on that person's behalf for wrongful imprisonment. This happened in the same Cuyahoga County court system Kevin was tried under. In the late 1990s, Sam Reese Sheppard attempted to sue Cuyahoga County for the wrongful imprisonment of his father, Dr. Sam Sheppard, in the case of the murder of his mother, Marilyn. Sam Reese Sheppard was determined to not have the standing to sue, but it brought back maybe the biggest criminal trial of the 1950s. In the late 1990s, I once had the opportunity to see the original crime scene photos in this case at a training seminar and hear of the new revelation they led to.

One day, researching Lisa's case later on, I revisited the idea of a civil wrongful death lawsuit and came across something generally known as a "discovery rule" with regards to wrongful death suits in Ohio. It generally states that the statute of limitations can be paused or tolled for a case where it can be shown that a party couldn't have reasonably known a cause of death. An example referred to was if later scientific testing could reveal a cause of death which wasn't apparent in the time before. It seemed to be targeted for medical-related deaths or cases of contamination, but I wondered if it could somehow apply to Lisa's case. If it could be established that a homicide victim was actually killed by someone else, could a wrongful death then be pursued against said parties, even decades later? If they had been misled, whether intentional or not, could the Pruett family pursue a wrongful death lawsuit to this day?

I remembered one day as a young police officer when our chief held up a flyer about a four-hour training seminar on giving death notices and asked if anyone was interested in going to it. Nobody's hand shot up, certainly not mine. There were many different training courses that we would have been very interested in going to, but the idea of such a somber duty certainly did not elicit any excitement from the crowd. Imagine being the police officer tasked with knocking on the door of the Pruett family late that night. Imagine having to break the news to a fellow person of the most devastating news.

It was time, about a year had gone by, and especially since there could be that possible loophole in the law that might allow a civil lawsuit, I drafted a letter to the Pruetts in the most respectful and empathetic manner I could. I had practiced this letter a number of times, having a premonition in my head since the beginning that nothing would be done and it would continue being my responsibility. I finally mailed the letter and a copy of my final report at the time to them. Sometime later, I received a letter in which my letter and report were returned to me with a message in which they wished not to be contacted anymore.

I felt awful for months for having reopened a wound. It took a long time to realize that I could never take away their pain, and it ultimately was not my fault; it was the fault of others. I hated myself a bit, but I hated everything I had found, I hated the whole mess, and hated that I was still in the middle of it. I will convey the Pruetts' wish for privacy to everyone, and I will honor it, and ask the others to do the same.

I had written a letter to the family of Kevin Young, as I felt as a private citizen, they deserved to know the things I had found. I was contacted back, and spoke at length with a member of Kevin's family. It was interesting to hear the perspectives from someone close to the case. Kevin's family is not concerned at all about having his name cleared. The Youngs have also circled their wagons, in a way, from what they were put through. They circled their wagons around always knowing Kevin's portion of the truth, that he was inside their residence with them that night. The relative I spoke to clearly said that Kevin was sitting beside them on the couch, playing video games at the time of the murder. They expressed a great deal of empathy and concern for Lisa Pruett and her family.

The revisiting of possible lawsuits brought up important questions. If a person released early from involuntary psychiatric care harmed someone or caused a death soon after their release, could the psychiatric care facility be sued? I wouldn't wager against there being at least one attorney who would think they could successfully sue a hospital system in that case. Could that concern have existed immediately in the aftermath of finding a person killed? If someone had an important, high-paying career in that same hospital system, might his career suffer if a large wrongful death lawsuit were filed against his employer due to the actions of a family member? I always wanted to know why Robert Dreifort was separated from his employment at the Cleveland Clinic at the time of Kevin's trial. Susan Lape came forward with her recollections of Kevin's "confessions" in July 1991 after the press conference. Nothing was taken to a grand jury until fall of 1992, at least fifteen months later, after the general statute of limitations for a wrongful death lawsuit had expired.

CHAPTER 21: JUSTICE FROM SACRIFICE

This book is written for the memory of two people, and should serve as testament to the truth of both. Countless words have been said on screen and in print about them, thousands upon thousands of pages can be found. I wanted to cut to the truth for them, find out which words mattered, what was truth and what was not.

Lisa Pruett was truly a poetess, her seemingly endless expression of the things inside her is evident even looking through something as unromantic as court records. I did not read all of her notes and letters, but the ending of one caught me as I scrolled through screens of public records requests. She lamented the absence of her love, and wrote of the fear of coming down with pneumonia from taking walks alone in the rain. She affected the lives of others very positively and was a bright light in this world.

Lisa went looking for her love late one night. She was a Juliet looking for her Romeo. What she encountered was a Brutus. Evidence shows it was some blend of the Brutus of Shakespearean tragedy, and quite possibly that of her era's World Wrestling Federation (now World Wrestling Entertainment). I believe it can be established to a criminal jury in a court of law that a pair of common scissors was thrust into the upper left section of her back, puncturing her upper lung. Simple demonstrations on a piece of fruit with opened scissors will produce the same perforations as seen on photos of her shirt. Lisa was robbed of everything, every future moment of a good and long life. All those who knew and loved her were robbed of those things as well.

I also write this book for a young man standing on an overpass above Interstate 271, ready to jump to end his pain. He had just gone through the ordeal of an aggravated murder trial, the highest of crimes against another human being. Though a jury of his peers could not find him guilty of the crime, the betrayal of other segments of his society plagued him on that overpass, and would plague him the rest of his shortened life. Being a painter was not an artistic muse driving him, but the reality of a society who turned him into a virtual pariah. He was condemned to that from being on the front page of every newspaper and on every television news broadcast as the person to have committed a horrific crime on an innocent and lovely young teenage girl.

I wanted to understand what happened. I wanted to understand why it had to be Kevin.

Kevin Young was betrayed by many, possibly used by some. Photographs existed which should have called into question the accusations against him. Some certain photos of a pair of shoes should have put a halt to any accusations against him. The small details of these photos, though not easy to see, had the power to prevent his trial and end any suspicion against him. I cannot tell you who knew or did not know about these photos, or who did or did not know about the small but powerful potential details they showed. They were not found in the Cuyahoga County Prosecutor's Office files for the case. Kevin's defense attorney would not definitively answer if he had been given them or not. What we do have is a file with a "missing pictures" memo and a photo-developing envelope with a suspicious number of prints ordered. We also see the mention of scissors as a murder weapon disappear. After the first forty-eight hours of investigation, the murder weapon evolves to a pocketknife.

Kevin was not sent to prison, but still paid a high price the rest of his life for something evidence shows he had nothing to do with. I will finish a cause started by the late commentator Dick Feagler, and whose torch was picked up and furthered by journalist James Renner. If the previous words you have read in this book have not already, I hereby exonerate the late Kevin Young of any involvement in the death of Lisa Pruett. Not enough people asked questions, the right questions. I could never find an answer for why he had to be the suspect other than he just had to be. The rational mind suggests there is a possibility of a nefarious reason for that.

Kevin Young sacrificed, and the one thing we can now realize is possible out of his sacrifice is what we should have valued highest all along—justice for Lisa Pruett. Being finally charged and put through a sham of a trial put so many pictures and documents into public record under law. We have the ability now not only to know Kevin's truth, but to honor his sacrifice in being able to establish the truth of what happened to Lisa. Kevin's sacrifices can be used heroically.

I now resign from the case and hand it over to the people who may be able to bring justice in this case, you the public. I will specifically include the Cleveland area media in what I refer to as "the public," but the call is to anyone. Kevin and Lisa's pictures and names made many front pages and television broadcasts, and the media owe it to them to start asking the important questions and making demands. Dick Feagler is gone, and my best efforts have been ignored, and not because people don't take me seriously. If we don't care about the murder of a sixteen-year-old Girl Scout, then who do we care about as a society?

The Cleveland media needs to start making demands on the city of Shaker Heights. The blaming of Kevin Young was an illusion, a fraud perpetrated on a city, the justice system, and the public of Northeast Ohio. It is a mountain of a conflict of interest when Timothy Kohansky sits in command of an investigation in which his own father was involved in steering a homicide case towards Kevin Young, whether knowingly or unknowingly. It is a conflict of interest for a police department to be in charge of an investigation where there is a possibility their own former employees have criminal culpability. Too many people failed to ask questions. The media must demand that the Lisa Lee Pruett homicide investigation be turned over to an outside agency such as the Ohio Attorney General's Office or Cuyahoga County.

Justice is possible for the Poetess and the Painter, if we honor them and their sacrifices above such things as image and reputation. It started with a single picture of another tragic victim of murder, and ends with two pictures which tell the truth of Lisa Pruett and Kevin Young. These pictures both speak thousands of words, and can be more trustworthy than the millions of words found in reports, records, news archives, and any publication. These pictures need to be in front of a criminal grand jury.

At some point, not bringing this evidence before a grand jury should constitute a crime of accomplice after the fact in a homicide.

It is now up to you.

ACKNOWLEDGEMENTS

First and foremost, any accomplishments in the case are due to the lone efforts of journalist James Renner. Only one person was keeping this case alive over decades. His efforts in the media and in obtaining documents, pictures, and information were the most crucial things that could have been done. It does not matter if someone is mistaken about certain things; it matters that he was right about enough to make it an issue and a cause. It takes a lot to write a book, as I have learned, and I will respect, treasure, and recommend *Little, Crazy Children* the rest of my life.

I would also like to thank the following people and organizations: Richard Warner, for his guidance, encouragement, and being one of the few to truly help; Maureen Young, and her family, for the insight; the Cuyahoga County Prosecutor's Office; Dan Phillips for his inspirational song; the Mentor Public Library; Youngstown State University and the Y.S.U. Police Academy; the City of Kirtland; Elijah Toten and WildBlue Press for their faith and this opportunity; and my favorite former MPL and City of Kirtland employee, now heaven's hard-of-hearing security guard, Gene Volk.

For More News About Michael Kelly,
Signup For Our Newsletter:

http://wbp.bz/newsletter

Word-of-mouth is critical to an author's long-term success. If you appreciated this book please leave a review on the Amazon sales page:

https://wbp.bz/inpublicrecordr

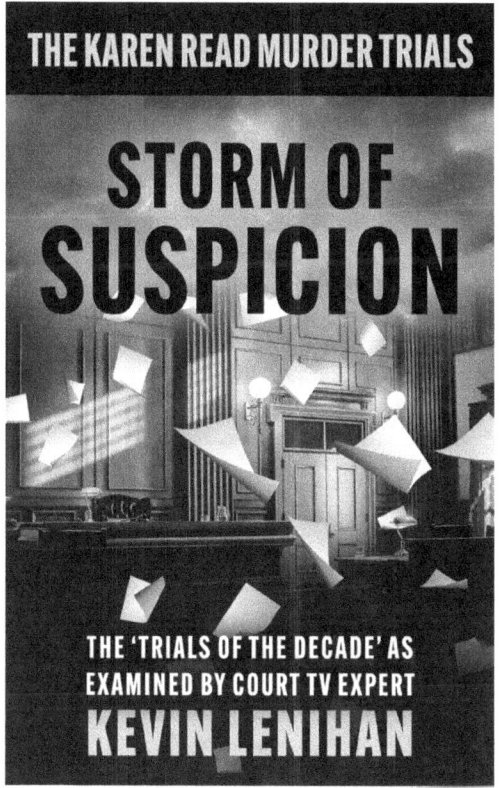

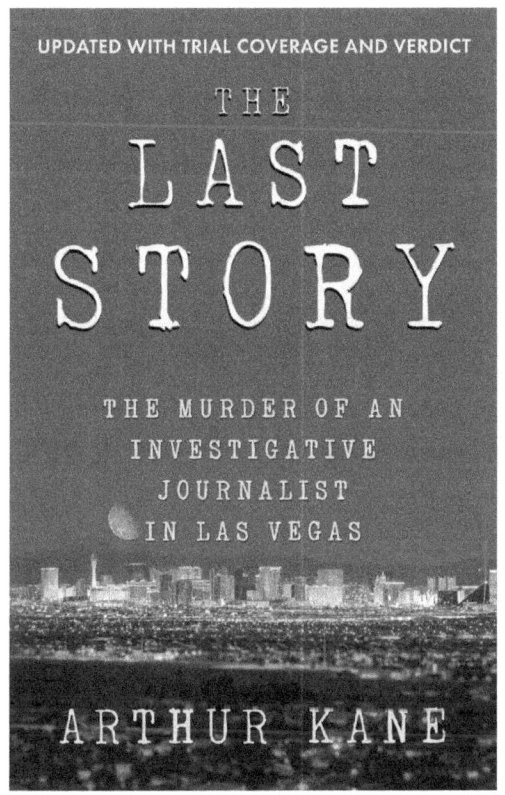

.